AIR FRYER COOKBOOK

*2000 Day Super Delicious, Quick & Easy
Air Fryer Recipes for Beginners, Family & Friends*

BY JONATHAN STIRLING

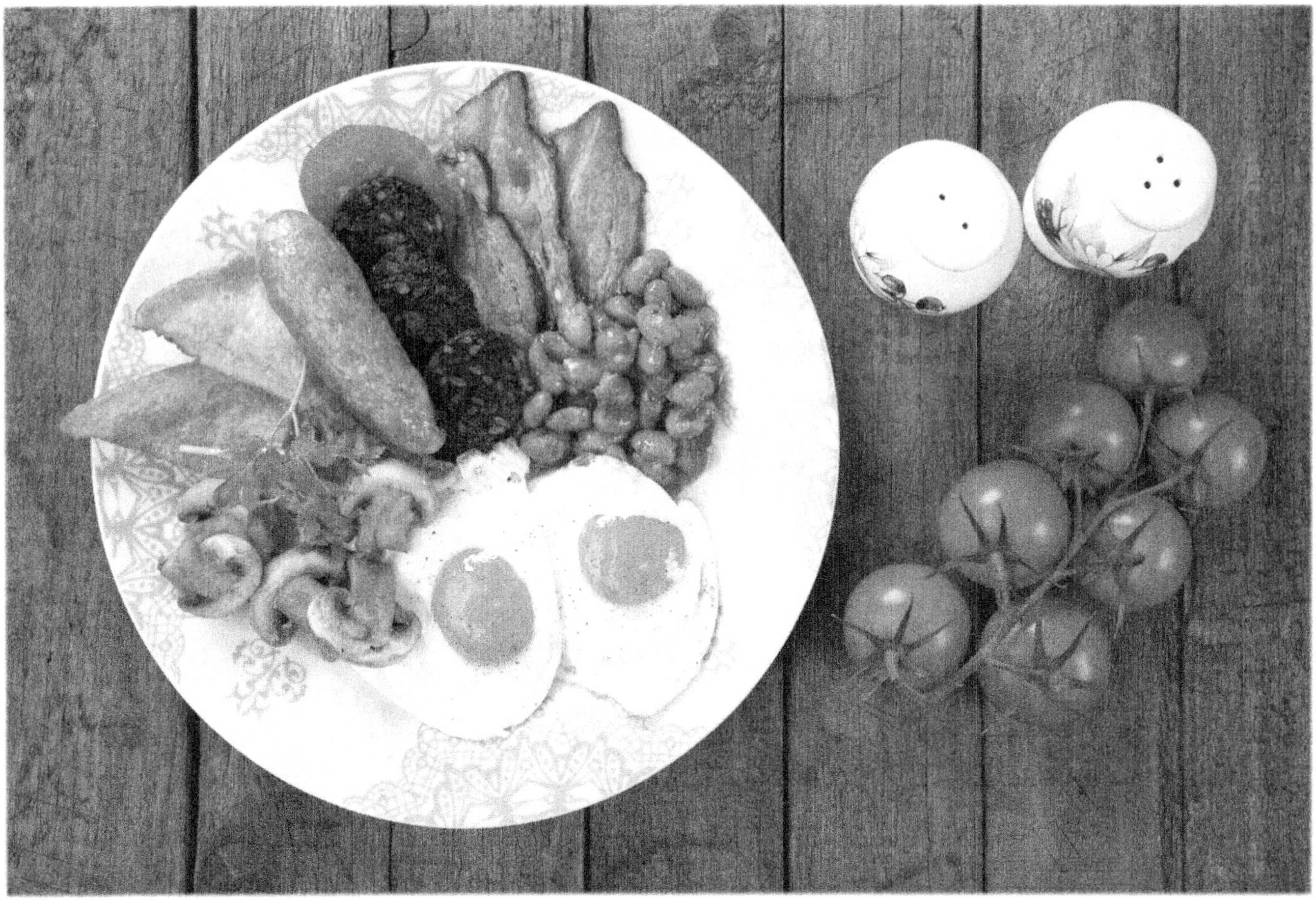

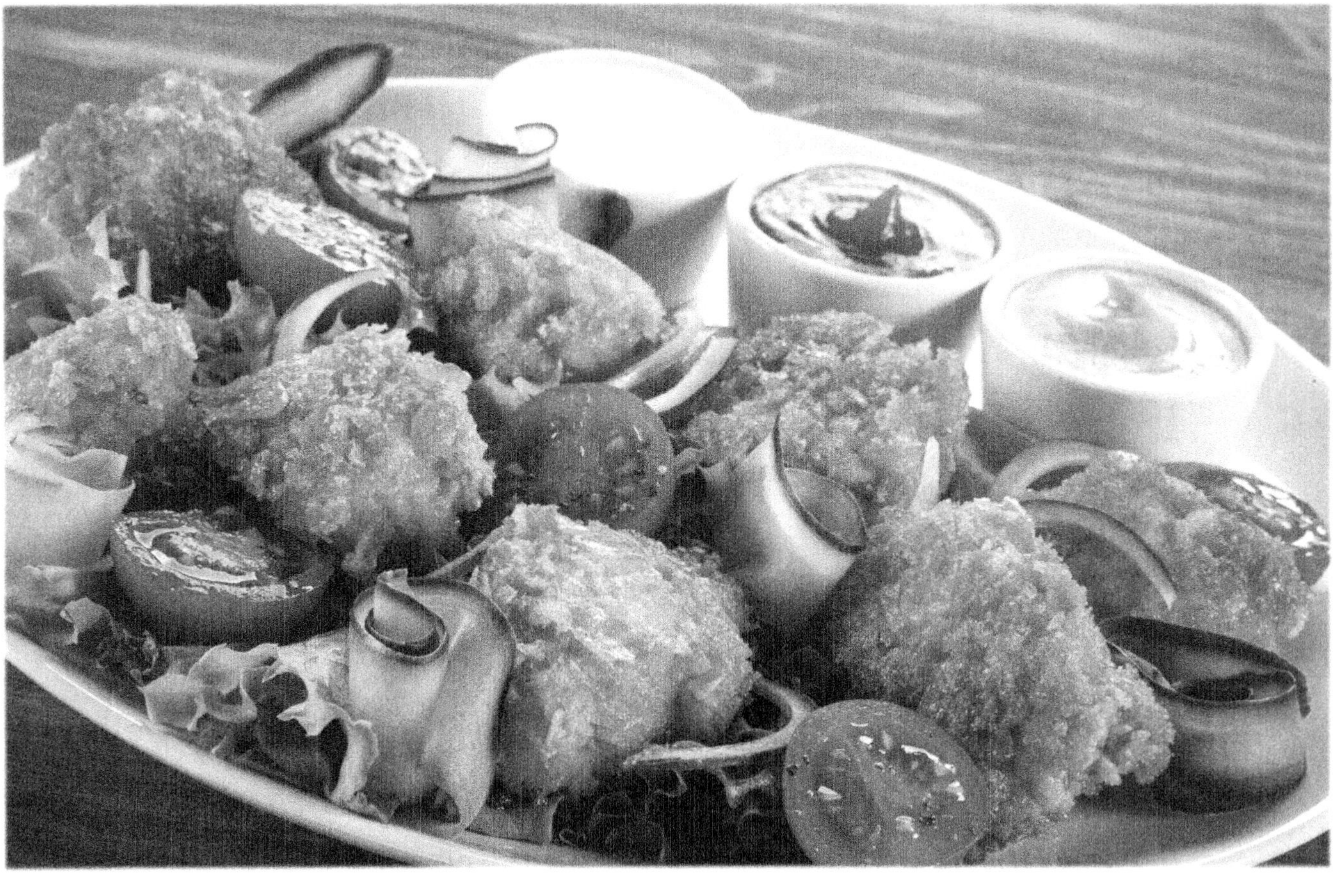

© **Copyright 2023 by Jonathan Stirling – All rights reserved.**

All rights reserved. No part of this publication or the information in it may be quoted from or reproduced in any form by means such as printing, scanning, photocopying or otherwise without prior written permission of the copyright holder.

Disclaimer and Terms of Use:

Effort has been made to ensure that the information in this book is accurate and complete, however, the author and the publisher do not warrant the accuracy of the information, text and graphics contained within the book due to the rapidly changing nature of science, research, known and unknown facts and internet. The Author and the publisher do not hold any responsibility for errors, omissions or contrary interpretation of the subject matter herein. This book is presented solely for motivational and informational purposes only.

TABLE OF CONTENTS

Introduction 1

What to Expect from Air Fryer Book..2

What Is an Air Fryer? 4

Air Fryer History..5

How Does the Air Fryer Work? 7

Benefits of Using an Air Fryer 9

Air Fryer Cooking Tips 11

Air Fryer Cleaning and Maintenance..14

Cooking Measurement Conversion Chart 16

BREAKFAST 19

Air Fryer Breakfast Burritos..19

Crispy Air Fried French Toast Sticks 20

Air Fryer Pancakes...21

Breakfast Sausage Links in the Air Fryer 22

Air Fryer Omelette..23

Hash Brown Patties in the Air Fryer 24

Air Fried Breakfast Potatoes 25

Blueberry Muffins in the Air Fryer...26

Cinnamon Sugar Donuts from the Air Fryer...27

Air Fryer Egg and Cheese Croissants 28

LUNCH 29

Air Fryer Grilled Cheese Sandwiches...29

Crispy Chicken Tenders in the Air Fryer 30

Air Fried Veggie Quesadillas..31

Air Fryer Tofu Nuggets 32

Air Fryer Falafel 33

Air Fryer Reuben Sandwiches 34

BBQ Pulled Pork in the Air Fryer 35

Air Fryer BLT Sandwich 36

Chicken Shawarma in the Air Fryer 37

Air Fried Crab Cakes 38

APPETIZERS AND SNACKS 39

Air Fryer Mozzarella Sticks 39

Crispy Air Fried Pickles 40

Air Fryer Buffalo Cauliflower Bites 41

Sweet Potato Fries from the Air Fryer 42

Air Fryer Stuffed Mushrooms 43

Jalapeño Poppers in the Air Fryer 44

Air Fried Onion Rings 45

Coconut Shrimp in the Air Fryer 46

Air Fryer Guacamole Dip 47

Crispy Air Fryer Zucchini Chips 48

DINNER 49

Air Fryer Steak with Garlic Butter 49

Air Fried Pork Chops 50

Lemon Herb Salmon in the Air Fryer 51

Air Fryer BBQ Ribs 52

Teriyaki Chicken Thighs in the Air Fryer 53

Air Fryer Shrimp Scampi 54

Cajun Blackened Catfish in the Air Fryer 55

Garlic Parmesan Chicken Wings from the Air Fryer 56

Air Fryer Meatloaf 57

Beef and Broccoli Stir-Fry in the Air Fryer 58

POULTRY 59

Air Fryer Chicken Tenders 59

Crispy Fried Chicken in the Air Fryer 60

Air Fryer Turkey Breast 61

Honey Mustard Glazed Chicken in the Air Fryer 62

Air Fried Chicken Parmesan 63

General Tso's Chicken from the Air Fryer 64

Air Fryer Chicken Fajitas 65

Buffalo Chicken Drumsticks in the Air Fryer 66

Lemon Pepper Wings from the Air Fryer 67

Air Fryer Chicken Cordon Bleu 68

SEAFOOD 69

Air Fryer Fish and Chips 69

Coconut-Crusted Shrimp in the Air Fryer 70

Garlic Butter Scallops in the Air Fryer 71

Air Fried Lobster Tails 72

Cajun Catfish Nuggets from the Air Fryer 73

Air Fryer Shrimp Po' Boys 74

Teriyaki Salmon in the Air Fryer 75

Lemon Garlic Butter Crab Legs from the Air Fryer 76

Air Fryer Tuna Steaks 77

Crispy Calamari in the Air Fryer 78

SIDE DISHES 79

Air Fryer Asparagus 79

Roasted Brussels Sprouts in the Air Fryer 80

Garlic Parmesan Air Fried Broccoli 81

Air Fryer Corn on the Cob 82

Sweet Potato Wedges in the Air Fryer 83

Air Fried Green Beans 84

Parmesan Zucchini Fries from the Air Fryer 85

Air Fryer Mac and Cheese Bites 86

Buffalo Cauliflower Wings in the Air Fryer 87

Air Fryer Garlic Bread 88

DESSERTS 89

Air Fryer Apple Fritters 89

Chocolate Lava Cakes from the Air Fryer 90

Air Fried Churros 91

Air Fryer Mini Cheesecakes 92

Cinnamon Sugar Air Fryer Donut Holes 93

Air Fryer S'mores 94

Banana Bread in the Air Fryer 95

Air Fried Oreos 96

Air Fryer Beignets 97

Peach Cobbler in the Air Fryer 98

Conclusion 99

INTRODUCTION

Step into the World of Air Frying!

If you've recently acquired an air fryer or are considering adding one to your kitchen, you're in for an exciting culinary adventure. This cookbook serves as your guide to exploring the vast array of culinary possibilities that an air fryer offers. Whether you're a seasoned cook or a kitchen newbie, this guide equips you with the knowledge and inspiration needed to elevate your cooking skills.

In this introductory section, we'll provide a sneak peek into what this air fryer cookbook has in store for you. From grasping the fundamental concept of air frying to exploring its history and scientific principles, we'll lay the foundation for a delicious journey. So, let's dive in and begin this flavourful exploration together!

WHAT TO EXPECT FROM AIR FRYER BOOK

Unveiling the Culinary Adventure Ahead

In this section, we'll offer you a glimpse of what this comprehensive air fryer cookbook entails. Consider it your roadmap to becoming an adept air frying enthusiast. We've thoughtfully curated an extensive range of recipes, insights, and techniques to ensure you maximise the potential of your air fryer. Here's a sneak peek at what awaits you:

A Diverse Array of Recipes

From crispy appetisers and mouthwatering main courses to delectable desserts, we've covered it all. Our cookbook boasts a varied collection of recipes that cater to diverse tastes and dietary preferences. Whether you're a carnivore, vegetarian, or have special dietary needs, you'll discover dishes that tantalise your taste buds.

Step-by-Step Instructions

Recognising that cooking can be intimidating, particularly with a new appliance, we've broken down each recipe into easy-to-follow steps. Whether you're an experienced chef or a novice, our instructions ensure that your dishes turn out flawlessly every time.

Cooking Insights and Hacks

We'll divulge invaluable tips and tricks to help you make the most of your air fryer. Learn how to achieve that irresistible crispiness, adapt traditional recipes to the air fryer, and much more. Our aim is to empower you with the knowledge to experiment and craft your air fryer creations.

Nutritional Understanding

Discover the health advantages of air frying compared to traditional deep-frying methods. We'll delve into how air frying allows you to reduce your oil consumption while still savouring crispy delights. It's a win-win for both your taste buds and your well-being.

Maintenance Wisdom

To ensure your air fryer's durability and optimal performance, we'll offer guidance on cleaning and maintenance. Proper care guarantees that your air fryer continues to serve up delightful meals for years to come.

With all this at your disposal, we're confident that you'll soon become a proficient air fryer chef. So, let's delve into the world of air frying!

WHAT IS AN AIR FRYER?

Unravelling the Mystery of Air Frying

Before we embark on our culinary journey, let's demystify the air fryer. What exactly is this kitchen appliance that has taken the culinary world by storm? In essence, an air fryer is a versatile kitchen gadget designed to emulate the results of deep frying without immersing food in oil. It accomplishes this through a combination of high-speed hot air circulation and a cooking basket, resulting in crispy, golden-brown deliciousness.

The Components of an Air Fryer

To grasp the essence of air frying, it's essential to acquaint yourself with its key components:

1. **Heating Element:** This element generates the heat needed for cooking. Typically located at the top of the air fryer, it emits intense radiant heat.
2. **Fan:** The fan is responsible for evenly distributing the hot air within the cooking chamber. It ensures that your food cooks uniformly and attains that coveted crispiness.
3. **Cooking Basket:** A removable basket is where you place your food items. It allows the hot air to circulate freely around the ingredients, cooking them evenly.
4. **Drip Tray:** Positioned below the cooking basket, the drip tray collects any excess oil or moisture that may drip from your food during cooking. This helps maintain healthier dishes and prevents smoking.
5. **Control Panel:** The control panel is where you set the cooking time and temperature. Most air fryers offer a range of temperature settings, typically between 180°C to 200°C (360°F to 400°F).

The Science Behind Air Frying

At the core of air frying lies the principle of convection cooking. Convection cooking relies on the circulation of hot air to transfer heat to your food. In the case of an air fryer, the heating element swiftly warms the air, while the fan ensures that this hot air constantly circulates around your food.

This hot air efficiently dehydrates the outer layer of your food, creating that irresistible crispy texture. Simultaneously, the interior cooks through conduction as the heat permeates the food. The outcome is a crispy exterior and tender interior, all achieved with significantly less oil than traditional deep frying.

Now that we've uncovered the inner workings of an air fryer, let's delve into its intriguing history in the next section.

AIR FRYER HISTORY

A Journey Through the Evolution of Air Frying

The concept of air frying, as we know it today, boasts a fascinating and storied history. It's a narrative of innovation, culinary ingenuity, and the quest for healthier cooking methods. In this section, we'll take you on a voyage through the evolution of air frying, from its modest origins to its current status as a kitchen essential.

Early Attempts at Healthier Frying

The desire to savour fried foods without the guilt of excessive oil consumption has deep roots dating back many decades. In the mid-20th century, several inventors and culinary enthusiasts began experimenting with various methods to achieve healthier frying.

One of the first inventors invented his own frying method in 1967. His invention utilised hot air and radiant heat to cook food with minimal oil. While not identical to today's air fryers, it laid the groundwork for future developments in air frying technology.

Emergence of the Air Fryer

The term "air fryer" as we recognise it gained traction in the early 2000s when various appliance manufacturers introduced kitchen gadgets that promised to replicate the taste and texture of deep-fried foods using hot air. These appliances piqued interest due to their potential for healthier frying without compromising on flavour.

While the precise timeline and credit for inventing the air fryer may be debated, it's clear that multiple companies and innovators contributed to its development. By the late 2000s, air fryers began gracing kitchens worldwide, revolutionising how people prepared their beloved fried dishes.

Continuous Advancements

Since the early models, air fryers have undergone significant enhancements in terms of technology, size, and functionality. Today's air fryers offer features such as digital displays, multiple cooking presets, and expanded cooking capacities, making them more versatile and user-friendly.

The popularity of air fryers has also spurred the creation of various accessories and cookbooks customised to this cooking method. This cookbook serves as a testament to the enduring appeal and culinary potential of air frying.

The Global Phenomenon

Air frying has transcended cultural and geographical boundaries, becoming a global sensation. Individuals from diverse backgrounds and cuisines have embraced air fryers as a convenient and healthier means to enjoy fried foods. The adaptability of this cooking method has stimulated culinary innovation, with cooks experimenting with dishes from around the world.

As we proceed to explore the subsequent chapters of this cookbook, you'll uncover how the air fryer can be your passport to savouring a world of flavours while preserving a healthier approach to cooking.

Now that we've traced the history of air frying, let's delve into the science behind how the air fryer works in the next section.

HOW DOES THE AIR FRYER WORK?

Demystifying the Magic of Hot Air Cooking

The air fryer's ability to produce crispy, golden-brown food with a fraction of the oil used in traditional deep frying might seem like culinary sorcery. However, in reality, it's all about harnessing the power of hot air and convection cooking. In this section, we'll take a closer look at how the air fryer achieves its culinary wizardry.

The Mechanics of Hot Air

At the core of the air fryer's operation lies the generation and circulation of hot air. Here's how it all comes together:

1. **Heating Element:** The air fryer's heating element, usually situated at the top of the appliance, is responsible for generating the heat necessary for cooking. It rapidly warms the air within the cooking chamber.
2. **Fan Action:** The fan plays a crucial role by drawing in the hot air and forcefully expelling it around the cooking chamber. This high-speed air circulation distinguishes air frying from conventional baking or roasting.
3. **Food Placement:** Your food is placed in a perforated basket within the cooking chamber. This design permits the hot air to reach all sides of the food, ensuring even cooking.

The Science of Convection

The fundamental principle behind air frying is convection cooking. Convection involves the transfer of heat through the movement of fluid, in this case, the movement of hot air. Here's how convection works within the air fryer:

1. **Dehydration:** The hot air swiftly removes moisture from the surface of your food. This dehydration process is what creates the crispy, golden crust that's characteristic of air-fried dishes.
2. **Crisping:** As the hot air circulates around your food, it consistently transfers heat to the surface. This leads to the Maillard reaction, a chemical process responsible for browning and flavour development. It's what imparts that irresistible crispiness to your food.
3. **Even Cooking:** The continuous circulation of hot air ensures that your food cooks uniformly on all sides. This eliminates the need to flip or rotate your dishes during cooking, saving you time and effort.

Reduced Oil Usage

One of the standout features of air frying is its ability to achieve deep-fried flavour and texture with significantly less oil. While traditional deep frying submerges food in a bath of hot oil, the air fryer relies on a thin coating of oil or none at all, making it a healthier alternative.

The combination of convection cooking and reduced oil usage not only results in crispy, delicious dishes but also reduces the overall calorie and fat content of your meals. It's a win-win for those seeking healthier eating options without sacrificing taste.

Now that you comprehend the science behind air frying, let's move on to explore the myriad benefits of incorporating an air fryer into your culinary repertoire.

BENEFITS OF USING AN AIR FRYER

Unveiling the Advantages of Air Frying

As you embark on your air frying journey, you'll swiftly realise the numerous benefits that this cooking method brings to the table. From health-conscious cooking to time-saving convenience, the advantages of using an air fryer are vast. In this section, we'll delve into the key benefits that make air frying a game-changer in the kitchen.

1. Healthier Culinary Choices

Arguably the most prominent advantage of air frying is its ability to reduce oil usage while still delivering that sought-after crispy texture. In contrast to deep frying, which submerges food in a pool of oil, the air fryer allows for similar results with only a fraction of the oil, rendering it a healthier choice.

2. Lower Fat Content

By using less oil, air frying significantly lowers the fat content of your dishes. This is particularly beneficial for individuals aiming to manage their weight or cut down on fat intake. You can indulge in your favourite fried foods with peace of mind, knowing you've made a healthier choice.

3. Versatile Cooking

Air fryers are remarkably versatile appliances. They can handle a wide spectrum of dishes, from crispy chicken wings and golden fries to roasted vegetables and even desserts. The capability to cook a variety of foods in a single compact device makes the air fryer a versatile kitchen ally.

4. Speedy Cooking Times

Air frying is renowned for its efficiency. The swift circulation of hot air guarantees that your food cooks rapidly and uniformly. Say goodbye to long preheating times and extended cooking sessions. With an air fryer, you'll have dinner ready in a fraction of the time required by traditional cooking methods.

5. Easy Cleanup

Cleaning up after cooking can be a chore, but air fryers simplify the process. Most models feature removable, dishwasher-safe components such as the cooking basket and drip tray. This translates to less time spent scrubbing pans and more time enjoying your meal.

6. Energy Efficiency

Air fryers are designed to be energy-efficient. They typically consume less electricity than traditional ovens or stovetop frying, making them an eco-friendly choice for cooking.

7. Customisable Recipes

Air fryers offer a wide range of temperature and time settings, providing you with control over your cooking. You can easily adapt recipes to suit your preferences, experimenting with different settings to attain your desired level of crispiness and doneness.

8. Minimal Odour

Unlike traditional frying methods, air frying generates minimal odour. You won't need to contend with the lingering scent of fried food in your kitchen, enhancing your overall cooking experience.

9. Reduced Risk of Accidents

Traditional deep frying can be hazardous, with the potential for hot oil splatters and burns. Air frying eliminates this risk, ensuring a safer cooking environment, particularly for those with limited culinary experience.

10. Family-Friendly Cooking

Air fryers are a hit with families. Kids adore the crispy treats that can be prepared with minimal fuss, while parents appreciate the healthier options air frying provides. It's a win-win for family mealtimes.

Now that we've explored the plethora of benefits of air frying, let's move on to some essential cooking tips to ensure you achieve the best results with your air fryer.

AIR FRYER COOKING TIPS

Mastering the Art of Air Frying

To become a true air fryer aficionado, it's essential to have some culinary tricks up your sleeve. In this section, we'll share a collection of valuable cooking tips and techniques that will elevate your air frying game to the next level. Whether you're a novice or an experienced air fryer user, these tips will help you achieve culinary excellence.

1. Preheat Your Air Fryer

Just like an oven, it's crucial to preheat your air fryer for consistent results. Preheating ensures that the cooking chamber is at the desired temperature when you begin cooking. Most air fryers offer a preheat function that simplifies this step.

2. Pat Your Ingredients Dry

For optimal crispiness, pat your ingredients dry with paper towels before placing them in the air fryer basket. Excess moisture can hinder the crisping process, so eliminating it is vital for achieving that perfect crunch.

3. Apply a Light Coating of Oil

While one of the benefits of air frying is reduced oil usage, a light coating of oil can enhance both the crispiness and flavour of your dishes. Consider using an oil sprayer to evenly distribute a small amount of oil over your ingredients.

4. Avoid Overcrowding the Basket

To ensure even cooking, steer clear of overcrowding the air fryer basket. Piling or overlapping ingredients can obstruct the circulation of hot air, resulting in uneven outcomes. If necessary, cook in batches to maintain proper spacing.

5. Shake or Flip

For dishes such as fries or nuggets, shaking the basket or flipping the food halfway through the cooking time can promote even crisping. Employ tongs or a spatula to turn the ingredients gently.

6. Experiment with Seasonings

Don't shy away from experimenting with various seasonings. Explore different herbs, spices, and marinades to craft unique flavours. Exercise caution with wet marinades, as excessive liquid can affect the crispiness.

7. Utilise Parchment Paper or Liners

To simplify cleanup, contemplate using parchment paper or air fryer liners in the basket. These aids prevent sticking and minimise the need for extensive scrubbing.

8. Verify for Doneness

It's crucial to check for doneness as you cook. Utilise a meat thermometer for meats and poultry to ensure they reach their desired internal temperatures. For other dishes such as vegetables or frozen foods, a quick taste test will suffice.

9. Monitor Delicate Foods

Foods such as pastries or items containing cheese can cook swiftly and may brown faster than expected. Keep a vigilant eye on delicate items to prevent overcooking or burning.

10. Adjust Temperatures and Times

Every air fryer model has its unique characteristics, so don't hesitate to adapt cooking temperatures and times to suit your appliance and preferences. Maintain a record of your adjustments for future reference.

11. Experiment and Enjoy

The beauty of air frying lies in its versatility. Don't be afraid to experiment with diverse recipes and techniques. Through experimentation, you'll unearth your personal air frying style and develop signature dishes.

12. Maintain Cleanliness

Proper maintenance guarantees your air fryer's continued peak performance. Routinely clean the cooking basket, drip tray, and any other removable components as per the manufacturer's instructions. This prevents any build-up that could affect cooking performance.

By incorporating these tips into your air frying routine, you'll be well on your way to creating delectable, crispy dishes that will impress your family and friends. Now, let's proceed to a crucial aspect of air fryer ownership: cleaning and maintenance.

AIR FRYER CLEANING AND MAINTENANCE

Caring for Your Culinary Companion

To ensure your air fryer remains a reliable kitchen companion for years to come, proper cleaning and maintenance are essential. In this section, we'll guide you through the steps to keep your air fryer in pristine condition.

1. Unplug and Cool Down

Always unplug your air fryer before cleaning and allow it to cool down completely. The appliance's components can become exceptionally hot during cooking, so exercise caution.

2. Remove and Clean Removable Parts

Most air fryers come with removable components such as the cooking basket, drip tray, and sometimes a grill or rack. Remove these parts carefully and wash them with warm, soapy water. Depending on the manufacturer's instructions, these components may also be dishwasher-safe.

3. Clean the Interior

Wipe down the interior of the air fryer using a damp cloth or sponge. Pay particular attention to any stubborn food particles or grease. If needed, use a non-abrasive brush to gently scrub away persistent residues. Ensure no food debris remains inside the cooking chamber.

4. Clean the Heating Element and Fan

While the interior is accessible, take the opportunity to clean the heating element and fan. Utilise a soft brush or a can of compressed air to remove any accumulated dust or debris. A clean heating element and fan are critical for even cooking and odour prevention.

5. Wipe Down the Exterior

Don't forget to wipe down the exterior of your air fryer. Use a damp cloth to remove any grease or food splatters. Be careful not to let water enter the appliance's electrical components.

6. Empty the Drip Tray

Dispose of any liquid or oil collected in the drip tray. Rinse it thoroughly and allow it to dry before returning it to the air fryer.

7. Inspect the Power Cord

Examine the power cord for any damage or signs of wear and tear. If you notice any issues, contact the manufacturer to obtain a replacement cord. A damaged cord can pose a safety hazard.

8. Proper Storage

When not in use, store your air fryer in a cool, dry place. Ensure it's shielded from dust and moisture. If your air fryer has a detachable cord, store it separately to prevent tangling.

9. Routine Maintenance

Regularly conduct maintenance checks on your air fryer to ensure it operates correctly. This entails inspecting for loose or damaged parts and confirming that the heating element and fan are clean.

10. Consult the User Manual

Always consult your air fryer's user manual for precise cleaning and maintenance instructions. Different models may have unique requirements, so adhering to the manufacturer's guidelines is essential.

By following these cleaning and maintenance tips, you'll not only prolong the lifespan of your air fryer but also ensure it continues to deliver delightful results with each use.

COOKING MEASUREMENT CONVERSION CHART

Dry Measurements	
Measurement	Equivalent
1 pound	16 ounces
1 cup	16 tablespoons
3/4 cup	12 tablespoons
2/3 cup	10 tablespoons plus 2 teaspoons
½ cup	8 tablespoons
3/8 cup	6 tablespoons
1/3 cup	5 tablespoons plus 1 teaspoon
¼ cup	4 tablespoons
1/6 cup	2 tablespoons plus 2 teaspoons
1/8 cup	2 tablespoons
1/16 cup	1 tablespoon
1 tablespoon	3 teaspoons
1/8 teaspoon	Pinch
1/16 teaspoon	Dash
½ cup butter	1 stick of butter

Liquid Measurements	
Measurement	Equivalent (rounded for ease of use)
4 quarts	1 gallon
2 quarts	½ gallon
1 quart	¼ gallon
2 pints	1 quart
4 cups	1 quart
2 cups	½ quart
2 cups	1 pint
1 cup	½ pint
1 cup	¼ quart
1 cup	8 fluid ounces
3/4 cup	6 fluid ounces
2/3 cup	5.3 fluid ounces
½ cup	4 fluid ounces
1/3 cup	2.7 fluid ounces
¼ cup	2 fluid ounces
1 tablespoon	0.5 fluid ounces

U.S. to Metric Conversions	
U.S. Measurement	Metric Conversion (rounded for ease of use)
Weight Measurements	
1 pound	454 grams
8 ounces	227 grams
4 ounces	113 grams
1 ounce	28 grams
Volume Measurements	
4 quarts	3.8 liters
4 cups (1 quart)	0.95 liters
2 cups	473 milliliters
1 cup	237 milliliters
3/4 cup	177 milliliters
2/3 cup	158 milliliters
½ cup	118 milliliters
1/3 cup	79 milliliters
¼ cup	59 milliliters
1/5 cup	47 milliliters
1 tablespoon	15 milliliters
1 teaspoon	5 milliliters
½ teaspoon	2.5 milliliters
1/5 teaspoon	1 milliliter
Fluid Measurements	
34 fluid ounces	1 liter
8 fluid ounces	237 milliliters
3.4 fluid ounces	100 milliliters
1 fluid ounce	30 milliliters

Metric to U.S. Conversions	
Metric Measurement (rounded for ease of use)	U.S. Conversion
Weight Measurements	
500 grams	1.10 pounds
100 grams	3.5 ounces
50 grams	1.8 ounces
1 gram	0.04 ounces
Volume Measurements	
1 liter	0.26 gallons
1 liter	1.06 quarts
1 liter	2.1 pints

Metric to U.S. Conversions	
Metric Measurement (rounded for ease of use)	**U.S. Conversion**
1 liter	4.2 cups
500 milliliters	2.1 cups
237 milliliters	1 cup
177 milliliters	3/4 cup
158 milliliters	2/3 cup
118 milliliters	½ cup
100 milliliters	2/5 cup
79 milliliters	1/3 cup
59 milliliters	¼ cup
47 milliliters	1/5 cup
15 milliliters	1 tablespoon
5 milliliters	1 teaspoon
2.5 milliliters	½ teaspoon
1 milliliter	1/5 teaspoon
Fluid Measurements	
1 liter	34 fluid ounces
237 milliliters	8 fluid ounces
100 milliliters	3.4 fluid ounces
30 milliliters	1 fluid ounce

BREAKFAST

AIR FRYER BREAKFAST BURRITOS

Preparation: 15 minutes | **Cooking:** 10 minutes | **Total:** 25 minutes | **Yields:** 4 servings

Ingredients:

- 4 large eggs
- 2 tablespoons milk
- Salt and pepper for seasoning
- 4 large flour tortillas
- 4 cooked sausages, thinly sliced
- 1 cup cheddar cheese, grated
- 1/2 cup diced bell peppers
- 1/2 cup diced onions
- Cooking spray

Directions:

1. Whisk eggs, milk, salt, and pepper in a bowl.
2. Spoon the egg mixture onto tortillas, add sausages, cheese, bell peppers, and onions.
3. Fold and roll up the tortillas.
4. Preheat the air fryer to 180°C (360°F).
5. Coat burritos with cooking spray, then air fry for 10 minutes until golden and crisp.
6. Serve hot.

Nutritional Information (per serving):

Calories: 430 | Protein: 21g | Carbohydrates: 23g | Fat: 27g | Fiber: 2g

CRISPY AIR FRIED FRENCH TOAST STICKS

Preparation: 10 minutes | **Cooking:** 6 minutes | **Total:** 16 minutes | **Yields:** 4 servings

Ingredients:

- 4 slices of bread, cut into sticks
- 2 large eggs
- 60ml (1/4 cup) milk
- 1 teaspoon vanilla extract
- 1/2 teaspoon ground cinnamon
- 2 tablespoons sugar
- Cooking spray

Directions:

1. Whisk eggs, milk, vanilla, cinnamon, and sugar.
2. Dip bread sticks in the mixture.
3. Preheat the air fryer to 180°C (360°F).
4. Coat sticks with cooking spray and air fry for 6 minutes until golden.
5. Serve with syrup or jam.

Nutritional Information (per serving):

Calories: 180 | Protein: 7g | Carbohydrates: 28g | Fat: 4g | Fiber: 1g

AIR FRYER PANCAKES

Preparation: 5 minutes | **Cooking:** 8 minutes | **Total:** 13 minutes | **Yields:** 4 servings

Ingredients:

- 200g (1 1/2 cups) all-purpose flour
- 2 tablespoons sugar
- 1 tablespoon baking powder
- 1/2 teaspoon salt
- 240ml (1 cup) milk
- 1 large egg
- 2 tablespoons melted butter
- Cooking spray

Directions:

1. Mix flour, sugar, baking powder, and salt.
2. Whisk milk, egg, and melted butter.
3. Combine wet and dry ingredients.
4. Preheat the air fryer to 180°C (360°F).
5. Grease the basket, ladle pancake batter, and air fry for 8 minutes.
6. Serve with toppings.

Nutritional Information (per serving):

Calories: 290 | Protein: 8g | Carbohydrates: 46g | Fat: 8g | Fiber: 1g

BREAKFAST SAUSAGE LINKS IN THE AIR FRYER

Preparation: 2 minutes | **Cooking:** 10 minutes | **Total:** 12 minutes | **Yields:** 4 servings

Ingredients:

- 8 breakfast sausage links

Directions:

1. Preheat the air fryer to 180°C (360°F).
2. Place sausages in the basket.
3. Air fry for 10 minutes until browned.
4. Serve hot.

Nutritional Information (per serving):

Calories: 160 | Protein: 8g | Carbohydrates: 1g | Fat: 14g | Fiber: 0g

AIR FRYER OMELETTE

Preparation: 5 minutes | **Cooking:** 7 minutes | **Total:** 12 minutes | **Yields:** 2 servings

Ingredients:

- 4 large eggs
- Salt and pepper to taste
- 2 tablespoons milk
- 1/2 cup diced bell peppers
- 1/2 cup diced onions
- 1/2 cup cheddar cheese, grated
- Cooking spray

Directions:

1. Whisk eggs, milk, salt, and pepper.
2. Preheat the air fryer to 180°C (360°F).
3. Grease a dish with cooking spray, pour in the egg mixture.
4. Add bell peppers, onions, and cheese.
5. Place in the air fryer and cook for 7 minutes.
6. Slice into wedges and serve.

Nutritional Information (per serving):

Calories: 270 | Protein: 16g | Carbohydrates: 6g | Fat: 20g | Fiber: 1g

HASH BROWN PATTIES IN THE AIR FRYER

Preparation: 10 minutes | **Cooking:** 15 minutes | **Total:** 25 minutes | **Yields:** 4 servings

Ingredients:

- 4 medium potatoes, peeled and grated
- 1 small onion, finely chopped
- 2 tablespoons plain flour
- 1/2 teaspoon salt
- 1/4 teaspoon black pepper
- Cooking spray

Directions:

1. Squeeze moisture from grated potatoes.
2. Mix potatoes, onion, flour, salt, and pepper.
3. Preheat the air fryer to 200°C (390°F).
4. Shape patties and air fry for 15 minutes until golden.
5. Serve as a side dish.

Nutritional Information (per serving):

Calories: 140 | Protein: 3g | Carbohydrates: 30g | Fat: 1g | Fiber: 2g

AIR FRIED BREAKFAST POTATOES

Preparation: 10 minutes | **Cooking:** 20 minutes | **Total:** 30 minutes | **Yields:** 4 servings

Ingredients:

- 4 large potatoes, diced
- 2 tablespoons olive oil
- 1 teaspoon paprika
- 1/2 teaspoon garlic powder
- 1/2 teaspoon onion powder
- Salt and pepper to taste

Directions:

1. Toss potatoes, oil, paprika, garlic, onion, salt, and pepper.
2. Preheat the air fryer to 200°C (390°F).
3. Air fry for 20 minutes until crispy.
4. Serve as a breakfast side.

Nutritional Information (per serving):

Calories: 220 | Protein: 4g | Carbohydrates: 41g | Fat: 5g | Fiber: 4g

BLUEBERRY MUFFINS IN THE AIR FRYER

Preparation: 10 minutes | **Cooking:** 15 minutes | **Total:** 25 minutes | **Yields:** 6 servings

Ingredients:

- 150g (1 1/4 cups) all-purpose flour
- 100g (1/2 cup) granulated sugar
- 1 1/2 teaspoons baking powder
- 1/4 teaspoon salt
- 1/2 cup milk
- 1/4 cup vegetable oil
- 1 large egg
- 1 teaspoon vanilla extract
- 1 cup fresh blueberries

Directions:

1. Combine flour, sugar, baking powder, and salt.
2. Whisk milk, oil, egg, and vanilla.
3. Mix wet and dry ingredients, fold in blueberries.
4. Preheat the air fryer to 180°C (360°F).
5. Line silicone muffin cups.
6. Divide batter, air fry for 15 minutes.
7. Cool before serving.

Nutritional Information (per serving):

Calories: 270 | Protein: 4g | Carbohydrates: 42g | Fat: 10g | Fiber: 1g

CINNAMON SUGAR DONUTS FROM THE AIR FRYER

Preparation: 10 minutes | **Cooking:** 8 minutes | **Total:** 18 minutes | **Yields:** 4 servings

Ingredients:

- 200g (1 1/2 cups) all-purpose flour
- 100g (1/2 cup) granulated sugar
- 1 1/2 teaspoons baking powder
- 1/4 teaspoon salt
- 1/2 teaspoon ground cinnamon
- 120ml (1/2 cup) milk
- 1 large egg
- 2 tablespoons melted butter
- 1 teaspoon vanilla extract
- Cooking spray

For the cinnamon sugar coating:

- 50g (1/4 cup) granulated sugar
- 1 teaspoon ground cinnamon

Directions:

1. Combine flour, sugar, baking powder, salt, and cinnamon.
2. Whisk milk, egg, melted butter, and vanilla.
3. Mix wet and dry ingredients.
4. Preheat the air fryer to 180°C (360°F).
5. Grease the basket, drop spoonfuls of batter.
6. Air fry for 8 minutes until golden.
7. Coat with cinnamon sugar.
8. Serve warm.

Nutritional Information (per serving):

Calories: 370 | Protein: 6g | Carbohydrates: 69g | Fat: 8g | Fiber: 1g

AIR FRYER EGG AND CHEESE CROISSANTS

Preparation: 5 minutes | **Cooking:** 6 minutes | **Total:** 11 minutes | **Yields:** 2 servings

Ingredients:

- 2 croissants, split
- 2 large eggs
- Salt and pepper for seasoning
- 2 slices of cheddar cheese
- Cooking spray

Directions:

1. Preheat the air fryer to 180°C (360°F).
2. Grease the basket.
3. Whisk eggs, salt, and pepper.
4. Place croissant halves in the basket.
5. Pour egg mixture, add cheese slices.
6. Add top halves, air fry for 6 minutes.
7. Serve warm.

Nutritional Information (per serving):

Calories: 390 | Protein: 16g | Carbohydrates: 30g | Fat: 23g | Fiber: 1g

LUNCH

AIR FRYER GRILLED CHEESE SANDWICHES

Preparation: 10 minutes | **Cooking:** 5 minutes | **Total:** 15 minutes | **Servings:** 2

Ingredients:

- 4 slices of bread
- 4 slices of cheddar cheese
- 2 tablespoons softened butter

Directions:

1. Assemble cheese between bread slices.
2. Spread softened butter on sandwich exteriors.
3. Preheat air fryer to 180°C (360°F).
4. Place sandwiches in the air fryer basket.
5. Air fry for around 5 minutes, turning once, until they're golden and the cheese melts.
6. Serve hot and savor!

Nutrition Facts (per serving):

Calories: 390 | Protein: 14g | Carbohydrates: 28g | Fat: 26g | Fiber: 2g

CRISPY CHICKEN TENDERS IN THE AIR FRYER

Preparation: 20 minutes | **Cooking:** 12 minutes | **Total:** 32 minutes | **Servings:** 4

Ingredients:

- 500g (about 1 lb) chicken tenders
- 100g (1 cup) breadcrumbs
- 1 teaspoon paprika
- 1/2 teaspoon garlic powder
- Salt and pepper to taste
- 2 large eggs, beaten
- Cooking spray

Directions:

1. Coat chicken tenders in beaten eggs, followed by breadcrumb mixture.
2. Preheat air fryer to 200°C (390°F).
3. Lightly coat tenders with cooking spray.
4. Place them in the air fryer basket.
5. Air fry for approximately 12 minutes, flipping halfway, until they're crispy and golden.
6. Serve with your preferred dipping sauce.

Nutrition Facts (per serving):

Calories: 270 | Protein: 29g | Carbohydrates: 16g | Fat: 10g | Fiber: 1g

AIR FRIED VEGGIE QUESADILLAS

Preparation: 15 minutes | **Cooking:** 6 minutes | **Total:** 21 minutes | **Servings:** 2

Ingredients:

- 2 large whole wheat tortillas
- 100g (1 cup) grated cheddar cheese
- 1/2 red bell pepper, thinly sliced
- 1/2 green bell pepper, thinly sliced
- 1/2 red onion, thinly sliced
- 1 small zucchini, thinly sliced
- Cooking spray
- Salsa and sour cream (optional, for serving)

Directions:

1. Layer tortillas with cheese and sliced vegetables.
2. Preheat air fryer to 180°C (360°F).
3. Lightly coat quesadillas with cooking spray.
4. Place them in the air fryer basket.
5. Air fry for around 6 minutes until they're golden and cheese is melted.
6. Cut into wedges and serve with salsa and sour cream if desired.

Nutrition Facts (per serving):

Calories: 350 | Protein: 15g | Carbohydrates: 40g | Fat: 15g | Fiber: 6g

AIR FRYER TOFU NUGGETS

Preparation: 15 minutes | **Cooking:** 15 minutes | **Total:** 30 minutes | **Servings:** 4

Ingredients:

- 400g (14 oz) extra-firm tofu, cubed
- 2 tablespoons soy sauce
- 2 tablespoons cornstarch
- 1 teaspoon paprika
- 1/2 teaspoon garlic powder
- Cooking spray
- Sweet chili sauce (optional, for dipping)

Directions:

1. Marinate tofu in soy sauce.
2. Coat tofu in cornstarch mixture.
3. Preheat air fryer to 200°C (390°F).
4. Lightly coat tofu with cooking spray.
5. Place it in the air fryer basket.
6. Air fry for about 15 minutes, shaking the basket occasionally, until nuggets are crispy and browned.
7. Serve with sweet chili sauce for dipping.

Nutrition Facts (per serving):

Calories: 150 | Protein: 9g | Carbohydrates: 8g | Fat: 9g | Fiber: 1g

AIR FRYER FALAFEL

Preparation: 15 minutes | **Cooking:** 12 minutes | **Total:** 27 minutes | **Servings:** 4

Ingredients:

- 400g (14 oz) canned chickpeas, blended with spices
- 1 small red onion, chopped
- 2 cloves garlic, minced
- 2 tablespoons fresh parsley, chopped
- 1/2 teaspoon baking powder
- Salt and pepper to taste
- Cooking spray
- Tahini sauce (optional, for dipping)

Directions:

1. Mix chickpea mixture with onion, garlic, parsley, baking powder, salt, and pepper.
2. Preheat air fryer to 180°C (360°F).
3. Shape mixture into small patties.
4. Lightly coat falafel with cooking spray.
5. Place them in the air fryer basket.
6. Air fry for about 12 minutes, turning halfway through, until they're crispy and browned.
7. Serve with tahini sauce if desired.

Nutrition Facts (per serving):

Calories: 170 | Protein: 6g | Carbohydrates: 27g | Fat: 4g | Fiber: 6g

AIR FRYER REUBEN SANDWICHES

Preparation: 10 minutes | **Cooking:** 10 minutes | **Total:** 20 minutes | **Servings:** 2

Ingredients:

- 4 slices of rye bread
- 4 slices of Swiss cheese
- 200g (7 oz) cooked corned beef, thinly sliced
- 1/2 cup sauerkraut, drained
- 4 tablespoons Thousand Island dressing
- Softened butter

Directions:

1. Assemble sandwiches with cheese, corned beef, sauerkraut, and Thousand Island dressing.
2. Spread softened butter on sandwich exteriors.
3. Preheat air fryer to 180°C (360°F).
4. Place sandwiches in the air fryer basket.
5. Air fry for around 10 minutes until they're golden and the cheese melts.
6. Slice and indulge in these delightful Reuben sandwiches.

Nutrition Facts (per serving):

Calories: 650 | Protein: 31g | Carbohydrates: 38g | Fat: 43g | Fiber: 4g

BBQ PULLED PORK IN THE AIR FRYER

Preparation: 10 minutes | **Cooking:** 15 minutes | **Total:** 25 minutes | **Servings:** 4

Ingredients:

- 500g (about 1 lb) pulled pork, mixed with barbecue sauce
- 4 hamburger buns
- Coleslaw (optional, for topping)

Directions:

1. Mix pulled pork with barbecue sauce.
2. Preheat air fryer to 180°C (360°F).
3. Place pulled pork mixture in the air fryer basket.
4. Air fry for approximately 15 minutes, stirring occasionally, until heated through.
5. Toast hamburger buns.
6. Serve pulled pork on the buns, with coleslaw if desired.

Nutrition Facts (per serving):

Calories: 490 | Protein: 28g | Carbohydrates: 54g | Fat: 18g | Fiber: 2g

AIR FRYER BLT SANDWICH

Preparation: 10 minutes | **Cooking:** 6 minutes | **Total:** 16 minutes | **Servings:** 2

Ingredients:

- 4 slices of bread
- 8 strips of bacon
- 2 leaves of lettuce
- 2 slices of tomato
- Mayonnaise

Directions:

1. Cook bacon until crispy, then drain on paper towels.
2. Preheat air fryer to 180°C (360°F).
3. Spread mayonnaise on one side of each bread slice.
4. Assemble sandwiches with bacon, lettuce, and tomato between two slices.
5. Place sandwiches in the air fryer basket.
6. Air fry for approximately 6 minutes until the bread is toasted.
7. Slice and savor these classic BLT sandwiches.

Nutrition Facts (per serving):

Calories: 420 | Protein: 12g | Carbohydrates: 30g | Fat: 27g | Fiber: 2g

CHICKEN SHAWARMA IN THE AIR FRYER

Preparation: 15 minutes | **Cooking:** 15 minutes | **Total:** 30 minutes | **Servings:** 4

Ingredients:

- 500g (about 1 lb) boneless chicken thighs, marinated and sliced
- 2 tablespoons olive oil
- A mix of aromatic spices
- 4 cloves garlic, minced
- Salt and pepper to taste
- 4 pita bread
- Tzatziki sauce, fresh veggies, and condiments (optional, for topping)

Directions:

1. Marinate chicken with spices, olive oil, garlic, salt, and pepper.
2. Preheat air fryer to 200°C (390°F).
3. Arrange chicken in the air fryer basket.
4. Air fry for approximately 15 minutes, turning occasionally, until cooked and browned.
5. Warm pita bread.
6. Serve chicken shawarma in pita with tzatziki sauce, fresh veggies, and condiments if preferred.

Nutrition Facts (per serving):

Calories: 380 | Protein: 28g | Carbohydrates: 25g | Fat: 19g | Fiber: 4g

AIR FRIED CRAB CAKES

Preparation: 15 minutes | **Cooking:** 12 minutes | **Total:** 27 minutes | **Servings:** 4

Ingredients:

- 250g (9 oz) lump crabmeat, drained and flaked
- 2 tablespoons mayonnaise
- 1 tablespoon Dijon mustard
- 1 egg
- 2 tablespoons fresh parsley, chopped
- 1 teaspoon Old Bay seasoning
- 1/2 teaspoon Worcestershire sauce
- Bread crumbs
- Cooking spray
- Lemon wedges (optional, for serving)

Directions:

1. Blend crabmeat, mayonnaise, Dijon mustard, egg, parsley, Old Bay seasoning, and Worcestershire sauce.
2. Shape mixture into crab cakes.
3. Preheat air fryer to 200°C (390°F).
4. Lightly coat crab cakes with cooking spray.
5. Place them in the air fryer basket.
6. Air fry for around 12 minutes until they're crispy and browned.
7. Serve with lemon wedges if desired.

Nutrition Facts (per serving):

Calories: 170 | Protein: 12g | Carbohydrates: 10g | Fat: 9g | Fiber: 1g

APPETIZERS AND SNACKS

AIR FRYER MOZZARELLA STICKS

Preparation: 20 minutes | **Cooking:** 8 minutes | **Total:** 28 minutes | **Servings:** 4

Ingredients:

- 200g (7 oz) mozzarella cheese sticks, halved
- 1 cup breadcrumbs
- 1/2 cup all-purpose flour
- 2 large eggs, beaten
- Cooking spray
- Marinara sauce (for dipping)

Directions:

1. Coat mozzarella sticks with flour, then immerse them in beaten eggs.
2. Roll them in breadcrumbs for even coverage.
3. Preheat the air fryer to 200°C (390°F).
4. Lightly apply cooking spray to the mozzarella sticks.
5. Arrange them in the air fryer basket.
6. Air fry for approximately 8 minutes until they turn golden and crispy.
7. Serve hot with marinara sauce for dipping.

Nutrition Facts (per serving):

Calories: 250 | Protein: 10g | Carbohydrates: 20g | Fat: 14g | Fiber: 1g

CRISPY AIR FRIED PICKLES

Preparation: 15 minutes | **Cooking:** 10 minutes | **Total:** 25 minutes | **Servings:** 4

Ingredients:

- 200g (7 oz) dill pickle slices
- 1/2 cup all-purpose flour
- 1 tsp paprika
- 1/2 tsp garlic powder
- 2 large eggs, beaten
- 1 cup breadcrumbs
- Cooking spray
- Ranch dressing (for dipping)

Directions:

1. Pat pickle slices dry with a paper towel.
2. Combine flour, paprika, and garlic powder in a bowl.
3. Dip pickle slices in the flour mixture, followed by the beaten eggs.
4. Coat them with breadcrumbs.
5. Preheat the air fryer to 200°C (390°F).
6. Lightly spray the pickles with cooking spray.
7. Place them in the air fryer basket.
8. Air fry for about 10 minutes until they're crispy.
9. Serve hot with ranch dressing for dipping.

Nutrition Facts (per serving):

Calories: 180 | Protein: 5g | Carbohydrates: 27g | Fat: 5g | Fiber: 2g

AIR FRYER BUFFALO CAULIFLOWER BITES

Preparation: 15 minutes | **Cooking:** 15 minutes | **Total:** 30 minutes | **Servings:** 4

Ingredients:

- 400g (14 oz) cauliflower florets
- 1/2 cup all-purpose flour
- 1 tsp garlic powder
- 1 tsp onion powder
- 1/2 cup buffalo sauce
- Cooking spray
- Ranch dressing (for dipping)

Directions:

1. Mix flour, garlic powder, and onion powder in a bowl.
2. Coat cauliflower florets with the flour mixture.
3. Preheat the air fryer to 180°C (360°F).
4. Lightly apply cooking spray to the cauliflower.
5. Arrange them in the air fryer basket.
6. Air fry for approximately 15 minutes until they're crispy.
7. Toss with buffalo sauce.
8. Serve hot with ranch dressing for dipping.

Nutrition Facts (per serving):

Calories: 130 | Protein: 3g | Carbohydrates: 25g | Fat: 1g | Fiber: 3g

SWEET POTATO FRIES FROM THE AIR FRYER

Preparation: 10 minutes | **Cooking:** 15 minutes | **Total:** 25 minutes | **Servings:** 4

Ingredients:

- 2 large sweet potatoes, cut into fries
- 2 tbsp olive oil
- 1 tsp paprika
- 1/2 tsp garlic powder
- Salt and pepper to taste
- Cooking spray

Directions:

1. Toss sweet potato fries with olive oil, paprika, garlic powder, salt, and pepper.
2. Preheat the air fryer to 180°C (360°F).
3. Lightly spray the fries with cooking spray.
4. Arrange them in the air fryer basket.
5. Air fry for about 15 minutes until they're crispy and golden.
6. Serve hot as a delightful side dish.

Nutrition Facts (per serving):

Calories: 160 | Protein: 2g | Carbohydrates: 25g | Fat: 6g | Fiber: 4g

AIR FRYER STUFFED MUSHROOMS

Preparation: 15 minutes | **Cooking:** 10 minutes | **Total:** 25 minutes | **Servings:** 4

Ingredients:

- 12 large white mushrooms, cleaned, and stems removed
- 100g (1/2 cup) cream cheese
- 50g (1/2 cup) grated Parmesan cheese
- 2 cloves garlic, minced
- 2 tbsp fresh parsley, chopped
- Salt and pepper to taste
- Cooking spray

Directions:

1. Combine cream cheese, Parmesan cheese, minced garlic, fresh parsley, salt, and pepper in a bowl.
2. Stuff mushroom caps with the cream cheese mixture.
3. Preheat the air fryer to 180°C (360°F).
4. Lightly spray the mushrooms with cooking spray.
5. Arrange them in the air fryer basket.
6. Air fry for about 10 minutes until they're tender and slightly browned.
7. Serve these delectable stuffed mushrooms as an appetizer.

Nutrition Facts (per serving):

Calories: 120 | Protein: 5g | Carbohydrates: 3g | Fat: 9g | Fiber: 1g

JALAPEÑO POPPERS IN THE AIR FRYER

Preparation: 15 minutes | **Cooking:** 10 minutes | **Total:** 25 minutes | **Servings:** 4

Ingredients:

- 8 fresh jalapeño peppers, halved and seeds removed
- 100g (1/2 cup) cream cheese
- 50g (1/2 cup) grated cheddar cheese
- 2 cloves garlic, minced
- Cooking spray
- Ranch dressing (for dipping)

Directions:

1. Blend cream cheese, cheddar cheese, and minced garlic in a bowl.
2. Fill jalapeño halves with the cream cheese mixture.
3. Preheat the air fryer to 180°C (360°F).
4. Lightly spray the jalapeño poppers with cooking spray.
5. Arrange them in the air fryer basket.
6. Air fry for about 10 minutes until they're tender and the cheese is melted.
7. Serve hot with ranch dressing for dipping.

Nutrition Facts (per serving):

Calories: 130 | Protein: 4g | Carbohydrates: 4g | Fat: 10g | Fiber: 1g

AIR FRIED ONION RINGS

Preparation: 15 minutes | **Cooking:** 10 minutes | **Total:** 25 minutes | **Servings:** 4

Ingredients:

- 2 large onions, cut into rings
- 1 cup all-purpose flour
- 1 tsp paprika
- 1/2 tsp garlic powder
- 2 large eggs, beaten
- 1 cup breadcrumbs
- Cooking spray
- Ketchup (for dipping)

Directions:

1. Combine flour, paprika, and garlic powder in a bowl.
2. Dip onion rings in the flour mixture, then in beaten eggs.
3. Coat them with breadcrumbs.
4. Preheat the air fryer to 200°C (390°F).
5. Lightly apply cooking spray to the onion rings.
6. Arrange them in the air fryer basket.
7. Air fry for about 10 minutes until they're crispy and golden.
8. Serve hot with ketchup for dipping.

Nutrition Facts (per serving):

Calories: 200 | Protein: 5g | Carbohydrates: 38g | Fat: 3g | Fiber: 2g

COCONUT SHRIMP IN THE AIR FRYER

Preparation: 20 minutes | **Cooking:** 10 minutes | **Total:** 30 minutes | **Servings:** 4

Ingredients:

- 200g (7 oz) large shrimp, peeled and deveined
- 1/2 cup shredded coconut
- 1/2 cup breadcrumbs
- 2 large eggs, beaten
- Cooking spray
- Sweet chili sauce (for dipping)

Directions:

1. Dip shrimp in beaten eggs.
2. Coat them with a mixture of shredded coconut and breadcrumbs.
3. Preheat the air fryer to 200°C (390°F).
4. Lightly apply cooking spray to the coconut shrimp.
5. Arrange them in the air fryer basket.
6. Air fry for about 10 minutes until they're crispy and golden.
7. Serve hot with sweet chili sauce for dipping.

Nutrition Facts (per serving):

Calories: 220 | Protein: 10g | Carbohydrates: 17g | Fat: 13g | Fiber: 2g

AIR FRYER GUACAMOLE DIP

Preparation: 10 minutes | **Cooking:** 5 minutes | **Total:** 15 minutes | **Servings:** 4

Ingredients:

- 2 ripe avocados, mashed
- 1 tomato, diced
- 1/2 red onion, finely chopped
- 1 clove garlic, minced
- 1 lime, juiced
- 1/4 cup fresh cilantro, chopped
- Salt and pepper to taste
- Tortilla chips (for dipping)

Directions:

1. Combine mashed avocados, diced tomato, chopped red onion, minced garlic, lime juice, cilantro, salt, and pepper in a bowl.
2. Preheat the air fryer to 180°C (360°F).
3. Place the guacamole in an oven-safe dish.
4. Air fry for about 5 minutes until it's slightly warm.
5. Serve with tortilla chips for a tasty dip.

Nutrition Facts (per serving):

Calories: 150 | Protein: 2g | Carbohydrates: 11g | Fat: 12g | Fiber: 6g

CRISPY AIR FRYER ZUCCHINI CHIPS

Preparation: 15 minutes | **Cooking:** 12 minutes | **Total:** 27 minutes | **Servings:** 4

Ingredients:

- 2 large zucchinis, thinly sliced
- 1/2 cup breadcrumbs
- 1/4 cup grated Parmesan cheese
- 1 tsp Italian seasoning
- 2 large eggs, beaten
- Cooking spray
- Marinara sauce (for dipping)

Directions:

1. Dip zucchini slices in beaten eggs.
2. Coat them with a mixture of breadcrumbs, grated Parmesan cheese, and Italian seasoning.
3. Preheat the air fryer to 200°C (390°F).
4. Lightly apply cooking spray to the zucchini chips.
5. Arrange them in the air fryer basket.
6. Air fry for about 12 minutes until they're crispy and golden.
7. Serve hot with marinara sauce for dipping.

Nutrition Facts (per serving):

Calories: 130 | Protein: 7g | Carbohydrates: 15g | Fat: 5g | Fiber: 2g

DINNER

AIR FRYER STEAK WITH GARLIC BUTTER

Preparation: 10 minutes | **Cooking:** 10 minutes | **Total:** 20 minutes | **Servings:** 2

Ingredients:

- 2 ribeye steaks (200g each)
- 2 tablespoons olive oil
- 2 cloves of garlic, minced
- 2 tablespoons of butter
- Salt and black pepper, to taste
- Fresh parsley for garnish

Directions:

1. Coat the steaks with olive oil, minced garlic, salt, and pepper.
2. Preheat the air fryer to 200°C (390°F).
3. Place the steaks in the air fryer basket.
4. Air fry for 10 minutes, turning them halfway for even cooking.
5. In a saucepan, melt the butter over low heat.
6. Pour the garlic butter over the cooked steaks.
7. Garnish with fresh parsley.
8. Serve while hot.

Nutrition Facts (per serving):

Calories: 450 | Protein: 30g | Carbohydrates: 1g | Fat: 36g | Fiber: 0g

AIR FRIED PORK CHOPS

Preparation: 15 minutes | **Cooking:** 12 minutes | **Total:** 27 minutes | **Servings:** 4

Ingredients:

- 4 pork chops
- 2 tablespoons olive oil
- 1 teaspoon paprika
- 1 teaspoon garlic powder
- Salt and black pepper, to taste

Directions:

1. Brush the pork chops with olive oil and season them with paprika, garlic powder, salt, and black pepper.
2. Preheat the air fryer to 190°C (375°F).
3. Place the pork chops in the air fryer basket.
4. Air fry for 12 minutes, flipping them halfway through for even cooking.
5. Serve hot with your preferred side dishes.

Nutrition Facts (per serving):

Calories: 280 | Protein: 30g | Carbohydrates: 1g | Fat: 17g | Fiber: 0g

LEMON HERB SALMON IN THE AIR FRYER

Preparation: 10 minutes | **Cooking:** 12 minutes | **Total:** 22 minutes | **Servings:** 2

Ingredients:

- 2 salmon fillets (150g each)
- 2 tablespoons olive oil
- Zest of 1 lemon
- 1 teaspoon dried thyme
- 1 teaspoon dried rosemary
- Salt and black pepper, to taste
- Lemon wedges for garnish

Directions:

1. Brush the salmon fillets with olive oil and season them with lemon zest, thyme, rosemary, salt, and black pepper.
2. Preheat the air fryer to 190°C (375°F).
3. Place the salmon fillets in the air fryer basket.
4. Air fry for 12 minutes until the salmon flakes easily with a fork.
5. Garnish with lemon wedges.
6. Serve hot with your choice of side dishes.

Nutrition Facts (per serving):

Calories: 350 | Protein: 28g | Carbohydrates: 2g | Fat: 25g | Fiber: 1g

AIR FRYER BBQ RIBS

Preparation: 10 minutes | **Cooking:** 40 minutes | **Total:** 50 minutes | **Servings:** 2

Ingredients:

- 500g pork ribs
- 1/2 cup barbecue sauce
- 1 teaspoon smoked paprika
- 1/2 teaspoon garlic powder
- Salt and black pepper, to taste

Directions:

1. Season the pork ribs with smoked paprika, garlic powder, salt, and black pepper.
2. Preheat the air fryer to 180°C (360°F).
3. Place the ribs in the air fryer basket.
4. Air fry for 40 minutes, turning and basting them with barbecue sauce every 10 minutes.
5. Serve hot with extra barbecue sauce.

Nutrition Facts (per serving):

Calories: 550 | Protein: 28g | Carbohydrates: 30g | Fat: 35g | Fiber: 1g

TERIYAKI CHICKEN THIGHS IN THE AIR FRYER

Preparation: 10 minutes | **Cooking:** 20 minutes | **Total:** 30 minutes | **Servings:** 4

Ingredients:

- 4 bone-in chicken thighs
- 1/2 cup teriyaki sauce
- 2 cloves garlic, minced
- 1 teaspoon ginger, minced
- 2 tablespoons sesame seeds
- Green onions for garnish

Directions:

1. Mix teriyaki sauce, minced garlic, and minced ginger in a bowl.
2. Brush the chicken thighs with the teriyaki mixture.
3. Preheat the air fryer to 190°C (375°F).
4. Place the chicken thighs in the air fryer basket.
5. Air fry for 20 minutes, turning them halfway through and brushing with more teriyaki sauce.
6. Sprinkle with sesame seeds and garnish with green onions.
7. Serve hot over rice or noodles.

Nutrition Facts (per serving):

Calories: 280 | Protein: 25g | Carbohydrates: 10g | Fat: 15g | Fiber: 0g

AIR FRYER SHRIMP SCAMPI

Preparation: 15 minutes | **Cooking:** 10 minutes | **Total:** 25 minutes | **Servings:** 4

Ingredients:

- 400g large shrimp, peeled and deveined
- 4 cloves garlic, minced
- 2 tablespoons olive oil
- Zest and juice of 1 lemon
- 1/4 cup fresh parsley, chopped
- Salt and black pepper, to taste
- Red pepper flakes for optional heat

Directions:

1. Mix shrimp, minced garlic, olive oil, lemon zest, lemon juice, and chopped parsley in a bowl.
2. Preheat the air fryer to 200°C (390°F).
3. Place the shrimp in the air fryer basket.
4. Air fry for 10 minutes, shaking the basket occasionally for even cooking.
5. Season with salt, black pepper, and red pepper flakes (if desired).
6. Serve hot with pasta or crusty bread.

Nutrition Facts (per serving):

Calories: 180 | Protein: 22g | Carbohydrates: 3g | Fat: 9g | Fiber: 1g

CAJUN BLACKENED CATFISH IN THE AIR FRYER

Preparation: 15 minutes | **Cooking:** 10 minutes | **Total:** 25 minutes | **Servings:** 4

Ingredients:

- 4 catfish fillets (150g each)
- 2 tablespoons Cajun seasoning
- 2 tablespoons olive oil
- Lemon wedges for garnish

Directions:

1. Brush the catfish fillets with olive oil and evenly sprinkle them with Cajun seasoning.
2. Preheat the air fryer to 190°C (375°F).
3. Place the catfish fillets in the air fryer basket.
4. Air fry for 10 minutes until they're blackened and cooked through.
5. Serve hot with lemon wedges.

Nutrition Facts (per serving):

Calories: 250 | Protein: 26g | Carbohydrates: 3g | Fat: 14g | Fiber: 1g

GARLIC PARMESAN CHICKEN WINGS FROM THE AIR FRYER

Preparation: 10 minutes | **Cooking:** 25 minutes | **Total:** 35 minutes | **Servings:** 4

Ingredients:

- 1 kg chicken wings
- 2 tablespoons olive oil
- 1/2 cup grated Parmesan cheese
- 2 cloves garlic, minced
- 1/2 teaspoon dried oregano
- Salt and black pepper, to taste
- Fresh basil leaves for garnish

Directions:

1. Toss the chicken wings with olive oil, grated Parmesan cheese, minced garlic, dried oregano, salt, and black pepper.
2. Preheat the air fryer to 200°C (390°F).
3. Place the chicken wings in the air fryer basket.
4. Air fry for 25 minutes, shaking the basket occasionally for even cooking.
5. Garnish with fresh basil leaves.
6. Serve hot with your choice of dipping sauce.

Nutrition Facts (per serving):

Calories: 380 | Protein: 30g | Carbohydrates: 2g | Fat: 28g | Fiber: 0g

AIR FRYER MEATLOAF

Preparation: 15 minutes | **Cooking:** 40 minutes | **Total:** 55 minutes | **Servings:** 4

Ingredients:

- 500g ground beef
- 1/2 cup breadcrumbs
- 1/4 cup milk
- 1/4 cup ketchup
- 1/4 cup diced onion
- 1/4 cup diced green bell pepper
- 1 egg
- 1 teaspoon Worcestershire sauce
- Salt and black pepper, to taste
- Cooking spray

Directions:

1. Mix ground beef, breadcrumbs, milk, ketchup, diced onion, diced green bell pepper, egg, Worcestershire sauce, salt, and black pepper in a bowl.
2. Shape the mixture into a loaf.
3. Preheat the air fryer to 180°C (360°F).
4. Place the meatloaf in the air fryer basket.
5. Air fry for 40 minutes until it's cooked through.
6. Allow it to rest briefly before slicing.
7. Serve hot with your favorite sides.

Nutrition Facts (per serving):

Calories: 350 | Protein: 20g | Carbohydrates: 15g | Fat: 23g | Fiber: 1g

BEEF AND BROCCOLI STIR-FRY IN THE AIR FRYER

Preparation: 15 minutes | **Cooking:** 10 minutes | **Total:** 25 minutes | **Servings:** 4

Ingredients:

- 400g beef sirloin, thinly sliced
- 2 cups broccoli florets
- 1/4 cup soy sauce
- 2 tablespoons oyster sauce
- 2 tablespoons brown sugar
- 2 cloves garlic, minced
- 1 teaspoon ginger, minced
- 1 tablespoon vegetable oil
- Sesame seeds for garnish
- Cooked rice for serving

Directions:

1. Combine soy sauce, oyster sauce, brown sugar, minced garlic, and minced ginger to make the sauce.
2. Brush beef slices with 2 tablespoons of the sauce.
3. Preheat the air fryer to 200°C (390°F).
4. Toss broccoli florets with vegetable oil and air fry for 5 minutes.
5. Add marinated beef to the basket and air fry for an additional 5 minutes, stirring occasionally.
6. Pour the remaining sauce over the beef and broccoli.
7. Air fry for 2 minutes until heated through.
8. Garnish with sesame seeds and serve hot over cooked rice.

Nutrition Facts (per serving):

Calories: 280 | Protein: 26g | Carbohydrates: 18g | Fat: 12g | Fiber: 2g

POULTRY

AIR FRYER CHICKEN TENDERS

Preparation: 15 minutes | **Cooking:** 12 minutes | **Total:** 27 minutes | **Servings:** 4

Ingredients:

- 500g chicken tenders
- 1 cup breadcrumbs
- 1/2 cup grated Parmesan cheese
- 1 teaspoon paprika
- 1/2 teaspoon garlic powder
- Salt and black pepper, to taste
- Cooking spray

Directions:

1. In a bowl, mix breadcrumbs, grated Parmesan cheese, paprika, garlic powder, salt, and black pepper.
2. Coat chicken tenders with the breadcrumb mixture.
3. Preheat the air fryer to 200°C (390°F).
4. Place the chicken tenders in the air fryer basket, ensuring they're not too close.
5. Air fry for 12 minutes, turning them halfway for even cooking.
6. Serve with your preferred dipping sauce.

Nutrition Facts (per serving):

Calories: 350 | Protein: 30g | Carbohydrates: 15g | Fat: 18g | Fiber: 1g

CRISPY FRIED CHICKEN IN THE AIR FRYER

Preparation: 20 minutes | **Cooking:** 20 minutes | **Total:** 40 minutes | **Servings:** 4

Ingredients:

- 8 chicken drumsticks
- 1 cup buttermilk
- 1 cup all-purpose flour
- 1 teaspoon paprika
- 1/2 teaspoon garlic powder
- Salt and black pepper, to taste
- Cooking spray

Directions:

1. Soak chicken drumsticks in buttermilk for 20 minutes.
2. In another bowl, mix flour, paprika, garlic powder, salt, and black pepper.
3. Preheat the air fryer to 200°C (390°F).
4. Dredge each drumstick in the flour mixture, pressing gently to adhere.
5. Place the drumsticks in the air fryer basket, making sure they're not crowded.
6. Air fry for 20 minutes, turning every 5 minutes for even cooking.
7. Serve with your preferred sides.

Nutrition Facts (per serving):

Calories: 350 | Protein: 25g | Carbohydrates: 25g | Fat: 15g | Fiber: 1g

AIR FRYER TURKEY BREAST

Preparation: 15 minutes | **Cooking:** 50 minutes | **Total:** 1 hour 5 minutes | **Servings:** 4

Ingredients:

- 1 turkey breast (about 1 kg)
- 2 tablespoons olive oil
- 1 teaspoon dried thyme
- 1 teaspoon dried rosemary
- 1 teaspoon garlic powder
- Salt and black pepper, to taste

Directions:

1. Rub the turkey breast with olive oil, dried thyme, dried rosemary, garlic powder, salt, and black pepper.
2. Preheat the air fryer to 180°C (360°F).
3. Place the turkey breast in the air fryer basket.
4. Air fry for 50 minutes, turning it halfway for even cooking.
5. Check the internal temperature, which should reach 75°C (165°F).
6. Allow it to rest for a few minutes before slicing.
7. Serve with gravy and your favorite accompaniments.

Nutrition Facts (per serving):

Calories: 250 | Protein: 30g | Carbohydrates: 1g | Fat: 12g | Fiber: 0g

HONEY MUSTARD GLAZED CHICKEN IN THE AIR FRYER

Preparation: 15 minutes | **Cooking:** 20 minutes | **Total:** 35 minutes | **Servings:** 4

Ingredients:

- 4 boneless chicken breasts
- 1/4 cup honey
- 2 tablespoons Dijon mustard
- 1 tablespoon olive oil
- 1 teaspoon garlic powder
- Salt and black pepper, to taste

Directions:

1. In a bowl, mix honey, Dijon mustard, olive oil, garlic powder, salt, and black pepper.
2. Brush the chicken breasts with the honey mustard mixture.
3. Preheat the air fryer to 190°C (375°F).
4. Place the chicken breasts in the air fryer basket.
5. Air fry for 20 minutes, flipping them halfway and brushing with more honey mustard glaze.
6. Serve with your choice of sides.

Nutrition Facts (per serving):

Calories: 300 | Protein: 25g | Carbohydrates: 20g | Fat: 10g | Fiber: 0g

AIR FRIED CHICKEN PARMESAN

Preparation: 15 minutes | **Cooking:** 20 minutes | **Total:** 35 minutes | **Servings:** 4

Ingredients:

- 4 boneless chicken breasts
- 1 cup breadcrumbs
- 1/2 cup grated Parmesan cheese
- 1 cup marinara sauce
- 1 cup shredded mozzarella cheese
- 1 teaspoon dried basil
- 1/2 teaspoon garlic powder
- Salt and black pepper, to taste

Directions:

1. In a bowl, combine breadcrumbs, grated Parmesan cheese, dried basil, garlic powder, salt, and black pepper.
2. Coat chicken breasts with the breadcrumb mixture.
3. Preheat the air fryer to 200°C (390°F).
4. Place the chicken breasts in the air fryer basket.
5. Air fry for 15 minutes, turning them halfway for even cooking.
6. Spoon marinara sauce over each chicken breast and top with shredded mozzarella cheese.
7. Air fry for an additional 5 minutes until the cheese is melted and bubbly.
8. Serve hot over cooked pasta.

Nutrition Facts (per serving):

Calories: 380 | Protein: 35g | Carbohydrates: 20g | Fat: 16g | Fiber: 2g

GENERAL TSO'S CHICKEN FROM THE AIR FRYER

Preparation: 20 minutes | **Cooking:** 15 minutes | **Total:** 35 minutes | **Servings:** 4

Ingredients:

- 500g boneless chicken thighs, cut into bite-sized pieces
- 1/4 cup cornstarch
- 1 tablespoon soy sauce
- 1 tablespoon hoisin sauce
- 1 tablespoon rice vinegar
- 1 tablespoon honey
- 1 teaspoon sesame oil
- 1/2 teaspoon ginger, minced
- 2 cloves garlic, minced
- Red pepper flakes, for optional heat
- Green onions and sesame seeds, for garnish

Directions:

1. Toss chicken pieces in cornstarch to coat.
2. Preheat the air fryer to 200°C (390°F).
3. Place chicken pieces in the air fryer basket, ensuring they're well spaced.
4. Air fry for 15 minutes, shaking the basket occasionally for even cooking.
5. In a saucepan, mix soy sauce, hoisin sauce, rice vinegar, honey, sesame oil, minced ginger, minced garlic, and red pepper flakes (if desired).
6. Heat the sauce until it thickens.
7. Toss cooked chicken pieces in the sauce.
8. Garnish with green onions and sesame seeds.
9. Serve hot over steamed rice.

Nutrition Facts (per serving):

Calories: 350 | Protein: 25g | Carbohydrates: 20g | Fat: 18g | Fiber: 1g

AIR FRYER CHICKEN FAJITAS

Preparation: 15 minutes | **Cooking:** 15 minutes | **Total:** 30 minutes | **Servings:** 4

Ingredients:

- 500g boneless chicken breasts, sliced
- 2 bell peppers, thinly sliced
- 1 onion, thinly sliced
- 2 tablespoons olive oil
- 2 tablespoons fajita seasoning
- Salt and black pepper, to taste
- Flour tortillas, for serving
- Sour cream, salsa, and guacamole, for garnish

Directions:

1. Toss chicken slices, bell peppers, and onion with olive oil and fajita seasoning.
2. Preheat the air fryer to 200°C (390°F).
3. Place the chicken and vegetable mixture in the air fryer basket.
4. Air fry for 15 minutes, stirring halfway for even cooking.
5. Season with salt and black pepper.
6. Serve the fajita mixture in warm flour tortillas.
7. Garnish with sour cream, salsa, and guacamole.

Nutrition Facts (per serving):

Calories: 350 | Protein: 25g | Carbohydrates: 20g | Fat: 18g | Fiber: 3g

BUFFALO CHICKEN DRUMSTICKS IN THE AIR FRYER

Preparation: 15 minutes | **Cooking:** 20 minutes | **Total:** 35 minutes | **Servings:** 4

Ingredients:

- 8 chicken drumsticks
- 1/2 cup buffalo sauce
- 2 tablespoons melted butter
- 1 teaspoon garlic powder
- Salt and black pepper, to taste
- Ranch or blue cheese dressing, for dipping

Directions:

1. Mix buffalo sauce, melted butter, garlic powder, salt, and black pepper in a bowl.
2. Coat chicken drumsticks with the buffalo sauce mixture.
3. Preheat the air fryer to 200°C (390°F).
4. Place the chicken drumsticks in the air fryer basket.
5. Air fry for 20 minutes, turning them halfway for even cooking.
6. Serve hot with ranch or blue cheese dressing for dipping.

Nutrition Facts (per serving):

Calories: 350 | Protein: 25g | Carbohydrates: 3g | Fat: 25g | Fiber: 0g

LEMON PEPPER WINGS FROM THE AIR FRYER

Preparation: 10 minutes | **Cooking:** 20 minutes | **Total:** 30 minutes | **Servings:** 4

Ingredients:

- 500g chicken wings
- 2 tablespoons olive oil
- Zest of 1 lemon
- 1 teaspoon black pepper
- 1/2 teaspoon garlic powder
- Salt, to taste
- Fresh parsley for garnish

Directions:

1. Toss chicken wings with olive oil, lemon zest, black pepper, garlic powder, and salt.
2. Preheat the air fryer to 200°C (390°F).
3. Place the chicken wings in the air fryer basket.
4. Air fry for 20 minutes, shaking the basket occasionally for even cooking.
5. Garnish with fresh parsley.
6. Serve hot with lemon wedges.

Nutrition Facts (per serving):

Calories: 350 | Protein: 25g | Carbohydrates: 2g | Fat: 25g | Fiber: 1g

AIR FRYER CHICKEN CORDON BLEU

Preparation: 20 minutes | **Cooking:** 20 minutes | **Total:** 40 minutes | **Servings:** 4

Ingredients:

- 4 boneless chicken breasts
- 4 slices ham
- 4 slices Swiss cheese
- 1/2 cup breadcrumbs
- 1/4 cup grated Parmesan cheese
- 1/2 teaspoon dried thyme
- 1/2 teaspoon garlic powder
- Salt and black pepper, to taste
- Cooking spray

Directions:

1. Flatten chicken breasts gently between plastic wrap.
2. Layer each chicken breast with a slice of ham and a slice of Swiss cheese.
3. Roll up the chicken and secure with toothpicks.
4. In a bowl, combine breadcrumbs, grated Parmesan cheese, dried thyme, garlic powder, salt, and black pepper.
5. Coat chicken rolls with the breadcrumb mixture.
6. Preheat the air fryer to 190°C (375°F).
7. Place the chicken rolls in the air fryer basket, seam side down.
8. Air fry for 20 minutes, turning them halfway for even cooking.
9. Serve hot with a creamy Dijon sauce.

Nutrition Facts (per serving):

Calories: 380 | Protein: 35g | Carbohydrates: 15g | Fat: 20g | Fiber: 1g

SEAFOOD

AIR FRYER FISH AND CHIPS

Preparation: 30 minutes | **Cooking:** 30 minutes | **Total:** 1 hour | **Servings:** 4

Ingredients:

- 4 white fish fillets (e.g., cod or haddock)
- 1 cup all-purpose flour
- 1 tsp baking powder
- 1/2 cup sparkling water
- Salt and pepper to taste
- Cooking spray
- 4 large potatoes, cut into fries
- Olive oil
- Lemon wedges and tartar sauce for serving

Directions:

1. Create a batter by mixing flour, baking powder, sparkling water, salt, and pepper.
2. Preheat the air fryer to 200°C (390°F).
3. Dip fish fillets into the batter and place them in the air fryer.
4. Spray the fillets lightly with cooking spray.
5. Toss potato fries with olive oil, salt, and pepper, and air fry them alongside the fish.
6. Serve with lemon wedges and tartar sauce.

Nutrition Facts (per serving):

Calories: 450 | Protein: 30g | Carbohydrates: 60g | Fat: 10g | Fiber: 6g

COCONUT-CRUSTED SHRIMP IN THE AIR FRYER

Preparation: 30 minutes | **Cooking:** 10 minutes | **Total:** 40 minutes | **Servings:** 4

Ingredients:

- 500g large shrimp, peeled and deveined
- 1 cup shredded coconut
- 1 cup breadcrumbs
- 2 beaten eggs
- Salt and pepper to taste
- Cooking spray
- Sweet chili sauce for dipping

Directions:

1. Create a coating mixture by combining shredded coconut and breadcrumbs.
2. Coat each shrimp with the mixture, then place them in the air fryer.
3. Spritz the shrimp lightly with cooking spray.
4. Air fry until golden and crispy.
5. Season with salt and pepper.
6. Serve with sweet chili sauce for dipping.

Nutrition Facts (per serving):

Calories: 350 | Protein: 25g | Carbohydrates: 25g | Fat: 18g | Fiber: 2g

GARLIC BUTTER SCALLOPS IN THE AIR FRYER

Preparation: 16 minutes | **Cooking:** 6 minutes | **Total:** 22 minutes | **Servings:** 4

Ingredients:

- 500g scallops
- 2 tbsp melted butter
- 2 cloves garlic, minced
- 1 tbsp chopped fresh parsley
- Salt and pepper to taste
- Lemon wedges for serving

Directions:

1. Create a garlic butter mixture by combining melted butter, minced garlic, chopped parsley, salt, and pepper.
2. Toss scallops in the mixture and place them in the air fryer.
3. Air fry until they're tender and succulent.
4. Serve with lemon wedges.

Nutrition Facts (per serving):

Calories: 180 | Protein: 25g | Carbohydrates: 2g | Fat: 8g | Fiber: 0g

AIR FRIED LOBSTER TAILS

Preparation: 25 minutes | **Cooking:** 10 minutes | **Total:** 35 minutes | **Servings:** 4

Ingredients:

- 4 lobster tails
- 2 tbsp melted butter
- 1 tsp paprika
- 1/2 tsp garlic powder
- Salt and black pepper to taste
- Lemon wedges for serving

Directions:

1. Split lobster tails, brush with melted butter, and season with paprika, garlic powder, salt, and pepper.
2. Place them in the air fryer and cook until they're succulent.
3. Serve with lemon wedges.

Nutrition Facts (per serving):

Calories: 150 | Protein: 25g | Carbohydrates: 1g | Fat: 6g | Fiber: 0g

CAJUN CATFISH NUGGETS FROM THE AIR FRYER

Preparation: 27 minutes | **Cooking:** 12 minutes | **Total:** 39 minutes | **Servings:** 4

Ingredients:

- 500g catfish nuggets
- 1/2 cup cornmeal
- 1 tbsp Cajun seasoning
- 1/2 tsp garlic powder
- Salt and black pepper to taste
- Cooking spray
- Lemon wedges for serving

Directions:

1. Create a coating mixture by mixing cornmeal, Cajun seasoning, garlic powder, salt, and black pepper.
2. Coat catfish nuggets with the mixture and air fry them until they're crispy.
3. Serve with lemon wedges.

Nutrition Facts (per serving):

Calories: 250 | Protein: 20g | Carbohydrates: 20g | Fat: 10g | Fiber: 2g

AIR FRYER SHRIMP PO' BOYS

Preparation: 30 minutes | **Cooking:** 10 minutes | **Total:** 40 minutes | **Servings:** 4

Ingredients:

- 500g large shrimp, peeled and deveined
- 1 cup breadcrumbs
- 2 tbsp Cajun seasoning
- 2 beaten eggs
- 4 baguette rolls
- Lettuce, tomato slices, mayonnaise for assembling

Directions:

1. Create a coating mixture by combining breadcrumbs and Cajun seasoning.
2. Coat each shrimp with the mixture and air fry until they're crispy.
3. Assemble Po' Boy sandwiches with lettuce, tomato slices, and mayonnaise.
4. Serve the shrimp in the sandwiches.

Nutrition Facts (per serving):

Calories: 450 | Protein: 30g | Carbohydrates: 40g | Fat: 18g | Fiber: 3g

TERIYAKI SALMON IN THE AIR FRYER

Preparation: 22 minutes | **Cooking:** 12 minutes | **Total:** 34 minutes | **Servings:** 4

Ingredients:

- 4 salmon fillets
- Teriyaki sauce, honey, rice vinegar, sesame oil, ginger, garlic, salt, and pepper for the marinade
- Green onions, sesame seeds for garnish

Directions:

1. Create a teriyaki marinade by combining teriyaki sauce, honey, rice vinegar, sesame oil, ginger, garlic, salt, and pepper.
2. Marinate salmon fillets and air fry until they're perfectly cooked.
3. Garnish with green onions and sesame seeds.

Nutrition Facts (per serving):

Calories: 350 | Protein: 25g | Carbohydrates: 18g | Fat: 18g | Fiber: 1g

LEMON GARLIC BUTTER CRAB LEGS FROM THE AIR FRYER

Preparation: 20 minutes | **Cooking:** 10 minutes | **Total:** 30 minutes | **Servings:** 4

Ingredients:

- Crab legs
- Lemon zest, melted butter, garlic, salt, black pepper, fresh parsley, lemon wedges

Directions:

1. Flavor crab legs by brushing them with lemon garlic butter.
2. Air fry until they're tender and full of flavor.
3. Serve with fresh parsley and lemon wedges.

Nutrition Facts (per serving):

Calories: 280 | Protein: 22g | Carbohydrates: 1g | Fat: 21g | Fiber: 0g

AIR FRYER TUNA STEAKS

Preparation: 23 minutes | **Cooking:** 8 minutes | **Total:** 31 minutes | **Servings:** 4

Ingredients:

- Tuna steaks
- Olive oil, soy sauce, lemon juice, oregano, garlic, salt, and pepper for the marinade

Directions:

1. Marinate tuna steaks and air fry them until they're cooked to perfection.
2. Serve with your choice of sides.

Nutrition Facts (per serving):

Calories: 250 | Protein: 30g | Carbohydrates: 2g | Fat: 13g | Fiber: 0g

CRISPY CALAMARI IN THE AIR FRYER

Preparation: 25 minutes | **Cooking:** 10 minutes | **Total:** 35 minutes | **Servings:** 4

Ingredients:

- Squid rings
- Breadcrumbs, paprika, garlic powder, salt, black pepper, cooking spray, lemon wedges

Directions:

1. Create a coating mixture by combining breadcrumbs, paprika, garlic powder, salt, and black pepper.
2. Coat squid rings with the mixture and air fry until they're crispy.
3. Serve with lemon wedges.

Nutrition Facts (per serving):

Calories: 280 | Protein: 25g | Carbohydrates: 30g | Fat: 6g | Fiber: 2g

SIDE DISHES

AIR FRYER ASPARAGUS

Prep: 5 mins | **Cook:** 10 mins | **Total:** 15 mins | **Servings:** 4

Ingredients:

- 400g fresh asparagus spears
- 1 tbsp olive oil
- Salt and pepper, to taste
- Zest and juice of 1 lemon
- Optional: Grated Parmesan cheese

Directions:

1. Trim asparagus ends.
2. Toss in olive oil, salt, and pepper.
3. Air fry at 200°C (390°F) for 8-10 mins.
4. Sprinkle with lemon zest and juice.
5. Optionally, add grated Parmesan cheese.

Nutrition Facts (per serving):

Calories: 40 | Protein: 2g | Carbs: 5g | Fat: 2g | Fiber: 2g

ROASTED BRUSSELS SPROUTS IN THE AIR FRYER

Prep: 10 mins | **Cook:** 15 mins | **Total:** 25 mins | **Servings:** 4

Ingredients:

- 500g Brussels sprouts, halved
- 2 tbsp olive oil
- Salt, pepper, 2 cloves garlic, minced
- 2 tbsp balsamic vinegar

Directions:

1. Toss Brussels sprouts with olive oil, salt, pepper, and garlic.
2. Air fry at 200°C (390°F) for 12-15 mins.
3. Drizzle with balsamic vinegar.

Nutrition Facts (per serving):

Calories: 80 | Protein: 3g | Carbs: 11g | Fat: 4g | Fiber: 4g

GARLIC PARMESAN AIR FRIED BROCCOLI

Prep: 10 mins | **Cook:** 10 mins | **Total:** 20 mins | **Servings:** 4

Ingredients:

- 400g broccoli florets
- 2 tbsp olive oil
- 3 cloves garlic, minced
- 2 tbsp grated Parmesan cheese
- Salt and pepper

Directions:

1. Toss broccoli with olive oil, garlic, Parmesan, salt, and pepper.
2. Air fry at 180°C (360°F) for 8-10 mins.

Nutrition Facts (per serving):

Calories: 70 | Protein: 3g | Carbs: 7g | Fat: 4g | Fiber: 3g

AIR FRYER CORN ON THE COB

Prep: 5 mins | **Cook:** 12 mins | **Total:** 17 mins | **Servings:** 4

Ingredients:

- 4 corn on the cob
- 2 tbsp butter
- Salt, pepper
- Fresh parsley (optional)

Directions:

1. Brush corn with butter, sprinkle salt and pepper.
2. Air fry at 180°C (360°F) for 10-12 mins.
3. Optionally, garnish with parsley.

Nutrition Facts (per serving):

Calories: 120 | Protein: 2g | Carbs: 15g | Fat: 7g | Fiber: 2g

SWEET POTATO WEDGES IN THE AIR FRYER

Prep: 10 mins | **Cook:** 15 mins | **Total:** 25 mins | **Servings:** 4

Ingredients:

- 2 large sweet potatoes, wedged
- 2 tbsp olive oil
- Seasonings: paprika, garlic powder, salt, pepper
- Optional: Fresh thyme

Directions:

1. Toss sweet potato wedges with olive oil and seasonings.
2. Air fry at 200°C (390°F) for 12-15 mins.
3. Optionally, garnish with fresh thyme.

Nutrition Facts (per serving):

Calories: 150 | Protein: 2g | Carbs: 24g | Fat: 6g | Fiber: 4g

AIR FRIED GREEN BEANS

Prep: 5 mins | **Cook:** 10 mins | **Total:** 15 mins | **Servings:** 4

Ingredients:

- 400g fresh green beans
- 1 tbsp olive oil
- Seasonings: garlic powder, onion powder, salt, pepper
- Optional: Grated Parmesan cheese

Directions:

1. Toss green beans with olive oil and seasonings.
2. Air fry at 200°C (390°F) for 8-10 mins.
3. Optionally, add grated Parmesan cheese.

Nutrition Facts (per serving):

Calories: 40 | Protein: 1g | Carbs: 4g | Fat: 3g | Fiber: 2g

PARMESAN ZUCCHINI FRIES FROM THE AIR FRYER

Prep: 10 mins | **Cook:** 10 mins | **Total:** 20 mins | **Servings:** 4

Ingredients:

- 2 large zucchinis, cut into fries
- Coating: grated Parmesan, breadcrumbs, oregano, salt, pepper
- Cooking spray
- Marinara sauce (optional)

Directions:

1. Coat zucchini fries, air fry at 200°C (390°F) for 8-10 mins.
2. Optionally, serve with marinara sauce.

Nutrition Facts (per serving):

Calories: 120 | Protein: 6g | Carbs: 13g | Fat: 6g | Fiber: 2g

AIR FRYER MAC AND CHEESE BITES

Prep: 15 mins | **Cook:** 10 mins | **Total:** 25 mins | **Servings:** 4

Ingredients:

- 2 cups cooked macaroni
- Cheese, breadcrumbs, milk, egg, paprika, salt, pepper
- Cooking spray

Directions:

1. Shape mixture into bite-sized balls, air fry at 200°C (390°F) for 8-10 mins.

Nutrition Facts (per serving):

Calories: 350 | Protein: 15g | Carbs: 40g | Fat: 15g | Fiber: 2g

BUFFALO CAULIFLOWER WINGS IN THE AIR FRYER

Prep: 15 mins | **Cook:** 15 mins | **Total:** 30 mins | **Servings:** 4

Ingredients:

- Cauliflower: 1 medium head, cut into florets (about 4 cups)
- Batter: 1 cup all-purpose flour mixed with 1 cup water (for coating)
- Buffalo sauce: 1/2 cup
- Ranch dressing: 1/4 cup (for serving)

Directions:

1. Dip cauliflower, air fry at 200°C (390°F) for 12-15 mins.
2. Toss in buffalo sauce, serve with ranch dressing.

Nutrition Facts (per serving):

Calories: 150 | Protein: 4g | Carbs: 27g | Fat: 3g | Fiber: 3g

AIR FRYER GARLIC BREAD

Prep: 5 mins | **Cook:** 5 mins | **Total:** 10 mins | **Servings:** 4

Ingredients:

- Baguette: 1 large, sliced
- Garlic: 2 cloves, minced
- Butter: 1/4 cup, softened
- Optional: Fresh parsley: 1 tablespoon, chopped (for garnish)

Directions:

1. Spread garlic butter on baguette, air fry at 180°C (360°F) for 3-5 mins.
2. Optionally, add fresh parsley.

Nutrition Facts (per serving):

Calories: 180 | Protein: 4g | Carbs: 25g | Fat: 7g | Fiber: 1g

DESSERTS

AIR FRYER APPLE FRITTERS

Prep: 15 mins | **Cook:** 10 mins | **Total:** 25 mins | **Servings:** 4

Ingredients:

- 2 peeled, cored, and diced apples
- 1 cup all-purpose flour
- 1/4 cup sugar
- 1 tsp baking powder
- 1/2 tsp cinnamon
- 1/4 tsp nutmeg
- A pinch of salt
- 1/2 cup milk
- 1 egg
- Vegetable oil for frying
- Powdered sugar for dusting

Directions:

1. Mix dry ingredients, then add wet ingredients and diced apples.
2. Preheat air fryer to 180°C (360°F).
3. Drop spoonfuls of batter into the air fryer.
4. Air fry until golden.
5. Dust with powdered sugar.

Nutrition Facts (per serving):

Calories: 280 | Protein: 5g | Carbs: 57g | Fat: 4g | Fiber: 3g

CHOCOLATE LAVA CAKES FROM THE AIR FRYER

Prep: 10 mins | **Cook:** 8 mins | **Total:** 18 mins | **Servings:** 4

Ingredients:

- Dark chocolate: 100g, melted
- Butter: 1/4 cup (about 56g), melted
- Flour: 1/4 cup (30g)
- Sugar: 1/4 cup (50g)
- Eggs: 2 large
- Vanilla extract: 1/2 teaspoon
- Optional: Fruit compote: 2 tablespoons (for topping)

Directions:

1. Combine melted chocolate and butter with other ingredients.
2. Preheat air fryer to 180°C (360°F).
3. Fill ramekins, air fry until set.
4. Cool, top with fruit compote if desired.

Nutrition Facts (per serving):

Calories: 450 | Protein: 6g | Carbs: 33g | Fat: 34g | Fiber: 2g

AIR FRIED CHURROS

Prep: 15 mins | **Cook:** 10 mins | **Total:** 25 mins | **Servings:** 4

Ingredients:

- Water: 1 cup
- Sugar: 2 tablespoons (for the dough)
- Flour: 1 cup
- Spices (such as cinnamon or nutmeg, if desired): 1/2 teaspoon
- Cinnamon sugar (for coating): 1/4 cup

Directions:

1. Make dough, preheat air fryer to 190°C (375°F).
2. Pipe dough into churros.
3. Air fry until golden.
4. Roll in cinnamon sugar.

Nutrition Facts (per serving):

Calories: 240 | Protein: 4g | Carbs: 34g | Fat: 10g | Fiber: 1g

AIR FRYER MINI CHEESECAKES

Prep: 15 mins | **Cook:** 15 mins | **Total:** 30 mins | **Servings:** 4

Ingredients:

- Cream cheese: 8 oz (225g), softened
- Sugar: 1/4 cup (50g)
- Eggs: 1 large
- Sour cream: 1/4 cup (60g)
- Vanilla extract: 1/2 teaspoon
- Graham cracker crumbs: 1/2 cup (for the base)
- Optional: Fruit compote: 2 tablespoons (for topping)

Directions:

1. Mix ingredients, line ramekins with crumbs.
2. Preheat air fryer to 160°C (320°F).
3. Air fry cheesecakes until set.
4. Cool, top with fruit compote if desired.

Nutrition Facts (per serving):

Calories: 350 | Protein: 6g | Carbs: 27g | Fat: 25g | Fiber: 0g

CINNAMON SUGAR AIR FRYER DONUT HOLES

Prep: 10 mins | **Cook:** 5 mins | **Total:** 15 mins | **Servings:** 4

Ingredients:

- Refrigerated biscuit dough: 1 can (about 8 biscuits)
- Sugar: 1/4 cup (for coating)
- Cinnamon: 1 teaspoon (for coating)
- Butter: 2 tablespoons, melted

Directions:

1. Cut dough, preheat air fryer to 180°C (360°F).
2. Brush with butter, roll in sugar-cinnamon.
3. Air fry until golden.

Nutrition Facts (per serving):

Calories: 220 | Protein: 2g | Carbs: 26g | Fat: 13g | Fiber: 1g

AIR FRYER S'MORES

Prep: 5 mins | **Cook:** 3 mins | **Total:** 8 mins | **Servings:** 4

Ingredients:

- Graham crackers: 4 whole crackers, broken in half to make 8 squares
- Chocolate: 4 small squares (one per s'more)
- Marshmallows: 4 large marshmallows

Directions:

1. Assemble s'mores, preheat air fryer to 180°C (360°F).
2. Air fry until marshmallows are gooey.
3. Enjoy!

Nutrition Facts (per serving):

Calories: 160 | Protein: 1g | Carbs: 34g | Fat: 3g | Fiber: 1g

BANANA BREAD IN THE AIR FRYER

Prep: 15 mins | **Cook:** 30 mins | **Total:** 45 mins | **Servings:** 4

Ingredients:

- Ripe bananas: 2 large, mashed
- Butter: 1/4 cup (56g), melted
- Sugar: 1/2 cup (100g)
- Eggs: 1 large
- Vanilla extract: 1 teaspoon
- Flour: 1 cup (125g)
- Baking soda: 1/2 teaspoon
- Optional nuts or chocolate chips: 1/4 cup

Directions:

1. Mix ingredients, preheat air fryer to 160°C (320°F).
2. Pour batter into a pan.
3. Air fry until a toothpick comes out clean.

Nutrition Facts (per serving):

Calories: 320 | Protein: 4g | Carbs: 51g | Fat: 12g | Fiber: 3g

AIR FRIED OREOS

Prep: 10 mins | **Cook:** 8 mins | **Total:** 18 mins | **Servings:** 4

Ingredients:

- Oreo cookies: 8 cookies
- Pancake batter: 1 cup (prepared according to package instructions)

Directions:

1. Dip Oreos, preheat air fryer to 180°C (360°F).
2. Air fry until crispy.

Nutrition Facts (per serving):

Calories: 200 | Protein: 2g | Carbs: 25g | Fat: 11g | Fiber: 1g

AIR FRYER BEIGNETS

Prep: 15 mins | **Cook:** 8 mins | **Total:** 23 mins | **Servings:** 4

Ingredients:

- Flour: 1 cup (125g)
- Sugar: 2 tablespoons
- Baking powder: 1 teaspoon
- Milk: 1/4 cup
- Egg: 1 large
- Vanilla extract: 1/2 teaspoon
- Powdered sugar: 2 tablespoons (for dusting)

Directions:

1. Mix ingredients, preheat air fryer to 180°C (360°F).
2. Drop spoonfuls of dough, air fry until golden.
3. Dust with powdered sugar.

Nutrition Facts (per serving):

Calories: 230 | Protein: 5g | Carbs: 46g | Fat: 2g | Fiber: 1g

PEACH COBBLER IN THE AIR FRYER

Prep: 15 mins | **Cook:** 25 mins | **Total:** 40 mins | **Servings:** 4

Ingredients:

- Sliced peaches: 2 cups (fresh or canned, drained)
- Sugar: 1/4 cup (50g)
- Flour: 1/2 cup (63g)
- Milk: 1/4 cup
- Baking powder: 1 teaspoon
- Salt: a pinch
- Optional: Vanilla ice cream: 1 scoop per serving (for topping)

Directions:

1. Mix ingredients, preheat air fryer to 160°C (320°F).
2. Bake until the top is golden.
3. Serve with vanilla ice cream if desired.

Nutrition Facts (per serving):

Calories: 300 | Protein: 4g | Carbs: 64g | Fat: 2g | Fiber: 2g

CONCLUSION

A Delicious Farewell

Congratulations! You've reached the conclusion of our air fryer cookbook, and we trust that this culinary voyage has been both enlightening and delectable. Equipped with the knowledge and techniques you've acquired, you're now well-prepared to make the most of your air fryer and explore its endless possibilities.

From crispy starters to succulent main courses and delightful desserts, the air fryer's versatility knows no bounds. Its ability to replicate the taste and texture of deep-fried delights with a fraction of the oil makes it a valuable addition to any kitchen.

Remember that cooking is an art, and mastering the air fryer is no different. Don't hesitate to experiment, adapt recipes, and craft your culinary masterpieces. Whether you're cooking for yourself, your family, or friends, the air fryer can be your trusted partner, streamlining meal preparation without compromising on flavour.

As you embark on your air frying adventures, keep in mind the benefits of this cooking method, including healthier meals, reduced cooking times, and the joy of experimenting with a wide range of dishes. Don't forget the invaluable cooking tips and cleaning and maintenance routines you've learned to keep your air fryer in impeccable condition.

Thank you for joining us on this flavourful journey through the world of air frying. May your air fryer continue to delight your palate and inspire your culinary creativity. Happy air frying, and bon appétit!

Printed in Great Britain
by Amazon